The World Regained

BY THE SAME AUTHOR

Donald Anderson: A Memoir (1966)
Arguing with my Grandmother (1973)
Frank Sargeson in his Time (1976)
Full of the Warm South (1983)
Presbyterians in Aotearoa: 1840–1990 (ed., 1990)
Shaking the Bee Tree (1992)
Then and There: a 1970s Diary (1995)
An Absurd Ambition: Autobiographical Writings: E. H. McCormick (ed., 1996)

THE WORLD REGAINED

DENNIS McELDOWNEY

AUCKLAND
UNIVERSITY
PRESS

First published by Chapman & Hall, London, 1957
This edition 2001

Auckland University Press
University of Auckland
Private Bag 92019
Auckland
New Zealand
http://www.auckland.ac.nz/aup

ISBN 1 86940 253 7

Cover design and illustration by Christine Hansen

Printed by Astra Print Ltd, Wellington

Introduction to the new edition

This account of illness, surgery and recovery was topical when it was first published in 1957, became dated, and is now period or even historical. Many incidental details taken for granted in the 1950s will now seem strange: an Auckland skyline dominated by the twin spires of churches and Norfolk pines rather than by high-rise buildings, a vehicular ferry instead of a bridge, a world where Christchurch airport's tiny terminal building was deserted for long stretches of the day, where deprived children lived in gender-segregated children's homes (though my father helped to change that), where young women were referred to as 'girls', and where 'he' was accepted as shorthand for 'he or she' even by women writers.

Much of the stay in hospital will still be familiar to people who have been in one recently, and it may even be a surprise to find that angiograms and heart catheterisations were done as early as 1950. But at that time the greater number of patients at Green Lane Hospital were tubercular, many of them in airy huts on the slopes of One Tree Hill (as described in Frank Sargeson's 'That Summer'), doctors were in no hurry to discharge patients from hospital and were apparently under no pressure to do so, and post-surgery recovery facilities were so primitive as to be almost non-existent. Within a decade, the operation described in this book, which was palliative rather than curative and still left a degree of disability, was replaced by the complete correction made possible by the development of the heart-lung machine. I had this second operation in 1961 and it opened the way to a career as a publisher and to marriage. Blue babies are still born (although they are seldom referred to as such), but there have not for a long time been any adult blue babies. Some still die when very young, but most are corrected by surgery before they are out of childhood.

Some aspects of hospital life in 1950 seemed so obvious that it didn't occur to me to mention them. Student nurses with few exceptions lived in the nurses' home attached to the hospital, were referred to by surnames only, and were liable to be paraded before the matron if male patients found out their first names. 'Oh, I am so *sorry*, Jo,' said one young nurse when she accidentally let slip a colleague's name while they were making a bed, and it was gleefully taken up by the thirty patients in the all-male ward; though it was also typical of the time that the men were careful not to use the name when a senior nurse was within hearing. The men spoke in two distinct vocabularies, one among themselves, the other in the presence of nurses and clergymen.

Nor did I mention what has since become my most pervasive memory of that time in Green Lane, the insistent zither of the Harry Lime theme from Carol Reed's film *The Third Man*, coming through all the hospital radios.

Beyond these historical curiosities I should like to think the core of the book is little affected by time. My intention was to convey what the confined world of an invalid looked like, its gradual opening out through the hospital experiences, and how strange, unexpected, exhilarating and frightening a larger world looked to one seeing it as a child would but through the eyes of an adult. The emphasis was intended to be on the World. The title was not accidental – though neither was the echo of *Paradise Regained.* After the book was published I was infuriated to find some libraries and bookshops shelving it among medical books.

Reading it for the first time for years I am conscious of some things I did not say, because they would have been difficult for me or impossible in the climate of the time. I was rather too upbeat about the experience of disability. I conveyed that to me it was natural and I was not unduly oppressed by it. But if this was so, why did I suck my thumb and distort my teeth, and go on sucking it secretly until I gave it up, cold turkey, just before my twenty-first birthday? My parents were aware, of course; but they believed I deserved some solace, and that it didn't matter much if I wasn't going to live long. As for the teeth, there were dentists in those days but no orthodontists, except perhaps for the very wealthy. The sight of so many adolescents going around with wire in their mouths would have seemed as bizarre then as any of the oddities of the earlier time do now. And it would have been impossible for anyone, outside perhaps of advanced psychological journals, to speak of an invalid adolescent's sexual needs and agonies. Even as it was, between the time of writing the book and its publication I became literally ill for a time worrying about the degree of self-revelation in it. I can see these things, but that does not mean I would write a better book now. Starting from scratch it would be impossible to recapture the exuberant sense of wonder. It is a young person's book.

I sometimes wonder about the management of my disability. I doubt whether nowadays bed-rest would be considered desirable treatment. It may also seem odd that I did not see a cardiologist from the age of four, when my condition was first (not fully) diagnosed, until twenty-four, when I went into Christchurch Hospital to be assessed for possible surgery at Green Lane. Both times, twenty years apart, it was the same cardiologist, Malcolm Gray. There were not many of them around. He could have done little, anyway. For the unarguable answer to such doubts is that at twenty-four, unlike most of those born with Fallot's tetralogy, I was still alive.

The 1950s have had a bad press. The decade is a by-word for dullness and conformity. It had a bad press even at the time, especially from the young writers with whom I aspired to associate. The penultimate paragraph of the book is an ironic comment on Bill Pearson's celebrated *Landfall* essay 'Fretful Sleepers' and other such writings. I couldn't agree with them, and it should be obvious from this book why. I had special reasons for finding the decade so exciting, but I never got over the suspicion that it could also have been exciting to anyone of a mind to be excited.

The World Regained began as a series of four radio talks with the same title delivered in 1952, as told in Chapter Twelve. Almost everything on radio was pre-scripted at the time, except Aunt Daisy. This enabled anything offensive or seditious to be removed. There was no national link (again except for Aunt Daisy); everything was done locally. Some recorded local programmes were picked up by head office and circulated round the country, so that weeks or months after it was first broadcast in Christchurch *The World Regained* still popped up in places like Gisborne and Greymouth. Its reception and the demand for cyclostyled copies of the scripts encouraged me to embark on a book. Not that I needed any encouragement: nothing would have held me back. I already thought of myself as a writer and had been presented with what seemed to me a perfect subject. The book was mostly written in 1954 and 1955. The text of the radio talks remained, but was scattered throughout.

This origin meant that the script was written for the ear. Even when expanding it into a book I was voicing it, though not in the sense of being chatty and colloquial. I tried to keep it lucid but at the same time enjoyed myself making up repetitive stylistic patterns and playing with the language, deliberately breaking the rules from time to time: 'an older folk out for an airing.' Some of this strikes me now as overdone, but I am not writing the book now. In the chapters written later the sentences became longer and more complex, under the unconscious influence of the Scott-Moncrieff translation of Proust, which I was reading at the urging of Frank Sargeson. Isobel Quigley in the London *Spectator* described the book as 'faintly Proustian', so there may be (faint) echoes of Proust in the content as well as the style. I am tempted to claim another source of my title in Proust's *Time Regained*, but *The World*

Regained had been used for the radio talks before I came to Proust.

When I finished and before looking for a publisher I asked Douglas Robb to check it for medical errors. 'In hospital,' I said, 'we learn most things by putting two and two together, and sometimes the answers we get just aren't so.'

'That's half the fun,' he replied, in conscious parody of the medical mystique he had tried hard to banish from Green Lane. 'We provide the mystery and we like to see what you make of it. It isn't really playing the game if we put you right.'

For whatever reason he didn't put anything right; but he did tell me I shouldn't bother with a local publisher. Douglas Robb's word was law to me at the time. He sent it to London himself, to his close friend Theodore Fox, editor of the *Lancet*, who agreed to act as honorary literary agent. After unsuccessfully trying some of the larger firms he placed it with Chapman & Hall, whose managing director happened to be his brother-in-law.

I was aware of Chapman & Hall largely as Dickens's publisher, and the connection thrilled me. I did not know that Chapman & Hall, by then part of the Heinemann group, had become almost exclusively a publisher of technical books with a very small general list. Their only notable author was Evelyn Waugh, who had stayed with them from loyalty and perhaps conservatism, his father having been an earlier managing director. When *The World Regained* came out it was advertised in the quality Sundays and weeklies in tandem with Waugh's novel based on his experience of hallucination, *The Ordeal of Gilbert Pinfold*, another connection which thrilled me. I don't know what Waugh thought about it. There were brief but kind reviews in a few of the London papers. Dan Davin wrote the one in the *Times Literary Supplement*, although since *TLS* reviews were unsigned it was years before I knew this. There were longer reviews in provincial papers, but it was naturally in New Zealand the book really featured, and most of the sales were in New Zealand. Publication in London was not to my financial advantage, since sales to New Zealand, regarded as export sales, carried a much lower royalty. There was also an American edition, published by the Beacon Press in Boston, a firm associated with the Unitarian Church. Their advance was generous, but their edition sank almost without trace. A photographic reprint of the Chapman & Hall edition with a brief new introduction was published in Dunedin by John McIndoe in Dunedin in 1976.

The text of this reissue is based on the original Chapman & Hall edition, except for the correction of the few misprints I found and of some errors of usage. I was not given the opportunity to read the proofs at the time, but except for some minor alterations to conform to their house style, Chapman & Hall followed my typescript faithfully, even where I now feel they should not have done. In that edition few of the people I wrote about were identified. Reasons for this reticence, if there were any reasons, have long since disappeared, and I have identified many in captions to illustrations or in endnotes, where I also comment on a few other matters which may seem curious. None of the previous editions was illustrated, so the pictures and the captions are new. But I have resisted the temptation to tinker with the text itself. As I have said, it is a young man's book, and it belongs rather to him than to me.

I am indebted to people who supplied photographs, particularly Peter Murray, Margaret Tripp and Mattie Wall. My apologies are due to copyright owners I was unable to trace. My thanks are due to Elizabeth Caffin for liking the book well enough to bring it back into print; to Katrina Duncan, who is not only a fine typographical designer but consults the author throughout the production process (as our email inboxes testify); to Christine O'Brien for energetic marketing; and to Annie Irving for holding the team together.

The original edition was dedicated to my parents and Douglas Robb. This one is dedicated to their memory.

One

Looking back, I find it difficult to credit. Nor, in fact, do I now look back very often, not with any intensity. I know, as one knows a date in history, that during my adolescence and early twenties I was increasingly bedridden; but it needs some special stimulus to bring those years back vividly, to recall to me what they meant, especially the last years, from 1947 – when I was twenty-one – until 1950, when my life had become so confined and uniform that I find it difficult to distinguish one year from another in my memory.

But occasionally memories will be shocked into life. When I find myself using the radio as a narcotic to lull me towards sleep at the end of a busy day, I sometimes remember a time when listening to the wireless was an exertion from which I had to rest after about half an hour, especially in the evening. I think it was in 1948 that the New Zealand stations broadcast the B.B.C. biography of Gilbert and Sullivan. They were outstanding programmes, and not what you would call strenuous listening. But each episode lasted an hour, they were broadcast from eight until nine, which was past my sleep-time, and in winter, which was never my best time. I listened to them all, and after each of them I lay awake for hours until the exhaustion and breathlessness passed off enough to let me sleep.

Those were the years, too, when the lists of books I had read – lists I kept assiduously – showed fewer and fewer titles. In the end I amalgamated the lists for two years, kept a *Reading list, 1948–9* instead of one for each of the two years, to try and make a better showing; and even so I could not muster more than twenty-four titles for the two years, and most of these were titles of very brief books, like George Orwell's *Animal Farm* and Evelyn Waugh's *The Loved One*. On a good day, when there were no interruptions, I could manage ten pages. I continued to buy books, for I had nothing else to spend my pocket-money on, and I acquired a collection of New Zealand poetry, among other things, which I am still pleased to find striking envy into the hearts of some of the few people who have the same interest; but the proportion of my books which I had myself read dropped lower each year.

The only work I did by then was for the Presbyterian Church weekly, *The Outlook*. The Editor, a determined person, had determined I should write for him on religious broadcasting. Therefore I wrote for him on religious broadcasting, a monthly article in which I gave my opinions about ministers on the air with what seems to me now to have been astonishing rudeness, and, as far as I can gather, delighted the ministry by doing it. I did not mention any of them by name, however. The articles, which averaged nine hundred words, I wrote slowly for half an hour each afternoon, wrote and re-wrote, and they consumed the whole of my physical and mental energy for the month, except that I might have a few days left at the end of the month's task in which to write letters.

I was always an object of solicitude to those who, knowing I had time on my hands, were anxious to fill it for me. They supplied me with enormous bundles of magazines. They made helpful suggestions about tatting, tapestry and basket-work. But in fact I seldom had time on my hands, or, rather, energy to spare; for time to do things is useless if there is no energy to do them with. I had reached a stage where the business of being alive, of eating, eliminating and keeping myself clean, absorbed almost all the energy I had. Even visitors were tiring if they came too often. As a naturally sociable person, I see-sawed between lamenting that not enough people came to see me, and, when my hopes were fulfilled, hoping they would not stay too long.

By rights I ought not to have been alive at all at that age, but since neither I nor anyone else knew it, I had gone on living. I had been born with a congenital heart condition known as Fallot's tetralogy. Fallot from the person who first described it; tetralogy because it consists of four related defects. The primary defect is a narrowing, or stenosis, in the pulmonary artery leading from the heart to the lungs. This means that the circulation of the blood to the lungs is deficient and that the blood does not receive enough oxygen to supply the necessary fuel for the muscles. The other three defects are secondary: they are attempts by the body to ensure that, in spite of the stenosis, the blood continues to circulate. But although they allow the blood to continue to flow they do little to increase the supply to the lungs, so there remain breathlessness and blueness, because of the insufficient oxygen. The effect on the victim is much the same as the effect of high altitudes on climbers. I have always had a fellow-feeling for Everest climbers when I have read of the miseries they suffer in those last few thousand feet, although I never attempted to climb a mountain when I was in that condition. In two further ways the body tries to make the best use of the available oxygen, and people who live in high altitudes, like the Indians in the Andes, adapt themselves in precisely the same way. The chest is over-developed to draw in as much air as possible, and the red corpuscles, whose job is to pick up oxygen in the lungs and carry it to the muscles, multiply enormously, so that whatever blood does reach the lungs can lift the greatest possible amount of oxygen.

This condition of pulmonary stenosis is popularly known as 'blue-baby' trouble – the genuine original blue-baby, though the name is loosely applied to a whole tribe of congenital conditions affecting the valves and walls inside the heart and the arteries leading from it. Many people react to the words 'blue-baby' by saying, 'Oh that's the thing where they change all the blood as soon as the baby's born'; but the Rh baby is a different matter altogether. The name blue-*baby* is significant, for until surgical help was developed few survived early childhood, and it was rare for any to be alive after the age of twenty-one, although it was by no means unknown. I have read of an American composer (whose name, as I had not heard it before, I promptly forgot) who, though a blue-baby, lived to his sixties. But it was against all probability that I should have been alive at twenty-four. Only, until I was twenty-four no one knew this.

It had been realised from the first that there was *something* wrong with my heart, and I gave my parents a pretty anxious time in my first few years. When I was four a heart specialist sent me for an electrocardiograph examination to the Christchurch hospital, an experience I remember vividly. The electrical contact was obtained in those days by dipping each hand and foot into a separate pot of water. This worried me considerably. I was afraid they might not have a towel handy to dry the hands and feet when the business was over.

The verdict disclosed the opening in the wall inside the heart, which was one of the secondary defects, but not the trouble outside, and this was what the doctors worked on for the next twenty years. It was more my fault than theirs, for I failed to conform to the symptoms of the true blue-baby. My symptoms, I was told when the truth was ultimately known, were cockeyed; and the most cockeyed of them all was that I was not noticeably blue, except after unusual exertion or excitement or when I got cold.

Meanwhile the doctor was quite cheerful – he thought I might live to about eight, with luck. Not that I knew anything about that, or about any of it; all I knew was that we suddenly and excitingly moved house. We moved from the house on the Cashmere hills which was the first I can remember and which had no flat land around it at all, to a house near the beach in Sumner, and it was in Sumner that I lived my childhood until I was eleven, a childhood which seems now to have been remarkably normal. I had already survived whooping-cough (at six months) and pneumonia (at three years). At Sumner I got through chicken-pox and measles and a few other ills, when I probably saw rather more of the local doctor than most children, a kind blunt man with bushy eyebrows and a bookcase in his surgery full of detective stories; but I was pretty healthy most of the time.

I began my schooling at Miss Pender's Preparatory School, which was almost a mile from where we lived and to which my mother wheeled me every morning in a pushchair. Miss Pender held her school in one of the rooms of a holiday-house belonging to St Saviour's Orphanage. Through the door was another, larger, darker room, crowded with tier upon tier of bunks; a room which would have been ideal for playing hide-and-seek if we had been allowed, which we weren't. We could only take an occasional tantalising glimpse through the door when Miss Pender's back was turned. Miss Pender's was a genteel institution. Miss Pender was six feet tall and charming, she looked after us beautifully, but I don't recall that anyone learned very much from her – except how to sing *All Things Bright and Beautiful,* which has remained my favourite hymn ever since. Miss Pender's was so genteel that I doubt if anyone there did anything which I could not do, and in spite of the fact that I arrived in a pushchair at an age when everybody else had grown out of such things I was a good deal less of an oddity than the unfortunate Pupsi, an Austrian boy (or he might have been Hungarian or Polish) whose mother made his hair grow long, like a girl's.

Even the pushchair wasn't *much* of an embarrassment, except when an occasional stranger would peer into it, surprised. But everyone I knew took it for granted, and so I did too. One of my friends, a small girl named Bobbie, who was four when I was six, wheeled me capably around most of Sumner in it. She once let her sister Mary, who was the same age as I, wheel me instead; but Mary landed me in the gutter, so I returned to the safer hands of Bobbie.

At seven, I graduated to a tricycle and the public school nearby. I started in the primers but only stayed there a term, which suggests that Miss Pender may have taught me something after all. When the class was lined up before marching in on the first day the teacher pointed me out and told the children they must take care of me. Every child turned and looked at me. I didn't like that at all, but I wasn't much oppressed. The only thing that really worried me on that first day was losing my slate-pencil. The school doctor came and was horrified to see me there. She wrote and underlined instructions about my treatment on my school card in red ink, forbade punishment, and told me I was never to go to school if I was tired, or if it was too hot or too cold – instructions I promptly forgot, and only know about because my mother lately told me. My attendance was erratic but I managed to keep my end up and to take part in many of the school activities. I didn't do the morning physical drill but I was very soon playing the radiogram for it, speeding up and slowing down *Colonel Bogey* as required. I recited by heart stories from Uncle Remus at afternoon penny concerts and once took part in a full-dress play in an evening concert, somewhat to the consternation of the teacher, who had cunningly made me *understudy,* and then had to give me the part when one of the principals left before the concert was put on. The teacher appeared at our house suddenly one lunch-time, an unheard-of thing, and while I returned to school she agreed with my mother that I might play one of the Goblins if I stayed in bed all day beforehand.

I was not allowed, on medical orders, to swim at the beach but I was allowed to paddle, and I interpreted this permission fairly liberally. When my knees began to hit the handle-bars of the tricycle I wanted a bicycle. The doctor and my parents were dubious but I forced their hands by saving up for it. They gave in and I rode it very sedately – most of the time.

I was conscious enough that I was not the same as other children, that I couldn't run as they could or climb trees or do anything very strenuous. When big boys had fights and everyone crowded around I kept on the outer rim of the circle, knowing I wouldn't have much chance if I got myself involved. But I spent little time regretting what I couldn't do; and when it came to exercising other than physical faculties I had no reason to hold back. I was an organiser. I organised the children of the neighbourhood in games, into impromptu concerts and fairs ('Fate' I wrote in chalk on the door of our backyard shed), into small adventures like putting pebbles on the tramline outside our gate, hiding behind the hedge, snickering, while the tram crunched them to powder, fearing, half hoping, the motorman would get down to investigate the cause of his rocky ride. I organised clubs which met under the weeping elm on our back lawn, wearing badges made of bottle-tops until some of the mothers objected to what they did to jerseys; while I as self-elected President kept a stern register of each member's conduct, marking against their names symbols ranging from B. to Ex. I'm afraid that often enough I was insufferably bossy, and thereby, possibly, compensated for any feelings of inadequacy which my physical limitations might have given me. Not that I can honestly say I remember having any such feelings, though what the unconscious mind was concluding I am not in a position to say.

I sometimes liked to go to Scarborough on my bicycle, past the boatsheds, where the unsinkable lifeboat, *Rescue II,* sat placidly waiting for the siren to herald one of Sumner's exciting moments, when a yacht would have capsized on the bar and the whole population would hurry to the beach to watch the *Rescue* go to the rescue. A fishing-boat might have been just drawn up on to the slip and men be unloading the glistening, bloody, fishy-smelling fish. I would walk further along the path and under the trees to a seat set into the cliff, grown around with orange-flowering ice-plants. There I would sit by myself and watch the waves breaking over the rocks. Paul Dombey also had this habit, it may be remembered, though it never occurred to me to ask what the wild waves might be saying. Looking back on these moments I sometimes like to imagine myself a solitary, sensitive, poetic child. But as soon as I have the picture in my mind I have sorrowfully to discard it, knowing I was far from poetic, not at all solitary, and not more sensitive than all children are, and a good deal less than some. The children I played with accepted my disability as naturally as I did, as naturally as my parents and my brother and sister did, and they never took an unfair advantage of it.

This was how things were until I was about twelve. But as adolescence approached I grew increasingly breathless, going to school became a drag and I grew reluctant to get up in the morning to face it. Finally I was kept home and enrolled with the Correspondence School whose lessons I did happily for several years, becoming a part of that remarkable organisation, which in spite of being carried on by post contrives to give its pupils the feeling of a corporate life, by the friendly personal letters from its teachers, its visiting teachers, its bulletins and magazines and radio programmes. A teacher in an ordinary school said to me once, 'A friend of mine teaches at the Correspondence School – at least she marks lessons, they don't *teach*,' which hurt my pride in my school even then, knowing they *did* teach, even at a distance, and often showed greater ingenuity than a classroom teacher had to do. I was even more annoyed when our daily paper took to referring to the Correspondence School in lower-case letters, 'correspondence school', alongside such respectably capitalised names as 'Technical College' and 'Boys' High School', thus evidently expressing its belief that my school was no real school at all.

As I went out less among people I peopled my room with a whole country of my own, drew maps of it, wrote its history, designed stamps for it, became myself any of its citizens I happened to fancy from day to day. Gradually, almost imperceptibly, my life closed in. I spent more and more time in bed, until I stayed there continuously. There was no uniform downward path: I would be very ill and then quite a lot better; there would be whole years when I was better than I had been; but the ups became less up and the downs further down. The efforts I made to pull myself out of the rut were less often successful, though I would not recognise it except as a temporary setback. I came to have so little energy for regular work that I had to give up the Correspondence School lessons; which was easier to do by then, for while my lack of energy had kept me behind with the assignments my brain had not lagged in proportion and I was struggling to complete work which had become too elementary. Nevertheless, though I gave the Correspondence School no academic distinction and have nothing to show from them but a primary school certificate, I owe them a lot.

Thereafter I acquired my own spasmodic education and thought myself to be doing pretty well, though I now find how many subjects I know nothing about, because they did not interest me at the time, which a school would have compelled me to learn. I learned not only from books but from the radio, which in a haphazard fashion feeds a regular listener with enough miscellaneous information and a showy enough vocabulary to let him converse with at least an appearance of learning. My family declared I learned even my accent from the B.B.C., though I denied this. I grew up, going quietly in my bed through the usual phases of religious doubt and left-wing enthusiasm. I carried on with a quarterly magazine which I wrote myself, and which indulgent friends duplicated for me (and for a time one even printed, on a handpress) and indulgent friends and relatives subscribed to; and this was my link with people at a time when I was less able to make new friends of my own and when, as my brother and sister married and left home, I could no longer share theirs. I grew out of this magazine eventually and killed it, and began to have a few articles and stories published in more-or-less adult publications; though this activity also declined with my energy until, apart from the *Outlook* articles, my literary activity was reduced to the odd letter-to-the-editor.

My life became a diminishing circle. Breathlessness kept me immobile, the immobility itself atrophied the muscles and reduced my activities still further; and all the time the breathlessness which set the whole downward progression going, grew worse. Yet there was nothing in my condition as it was known to deprive me of so much breath. The doctor was inclined to think it neurotic; I was inclined to agree with him; and although the explanation turned out to have been inadequate the doses of phenobarbitone he gave me did keep me quiet and helped me through several bad patches.

Blue-babies by the end of the forties were becoming news. The first regularly successful operations for relieving the condition were performed by Alfred Blalock and Helen Taussig at the Johns Hopkins Hospital in Baltimore from 1944. To the layman these operations were spectacular: the surgeon's knife was approaching the last inviolable region of the human body; and since it was extending the lives of children and young people they had a sentimental interest, so the newspapers kept us well informed about their progress. Before long cases were being sent from New Zealand to America for operation. Appeals were launched to raise funds for sending more, until it occurred to someone who had been concerned in one of the appeals that it would be more sensible to send a surgeon overseas to learn the technique. He led a deputation to the government: the government concurred and sent several deputations to persuade the leading thoracic surgeon in New Zealand to undertake the task. Reluctantly, because he already had as much work as he could cope with, he agreed. When he returned, in 1948, a cardio-surgical unit was set up at the Green Lane Hospital in Auckland and the first operations began for relieving Fallot's tetralogy, patent ductus, and coarctation of the aorta. The newspapers followed step by step. The Minister of Health watched one of the operations. Highly delighted by the experience she told an election meeting about it the same afternoon and made headlines throughout the country.

Which headlines I read, and all the other reports. The name of Green Lane began to represent a place where miracles were performed. But there was as yet no procedure for relieving any condition from which I was believed to be suffering, nor even an immediate prospect of one. So I waited, without really knowing I was waiting.

Two

And waited not unhappily. Related baldly the state of life I had reached sounds grim; but continuous unhappiness in any situation requires a strength of mind which I did not possess. My experience makes me doubt those who say that people who live under totalitarian regimes, who live in poverty, or without the enlightenment of modern civilisation, must all live in continual misery. I have no doubt that if they gave proper regard to their situation they ought to be wholly unhappy, but I am as convinced that, the frailty of human nature being what it is, they are unable fully to measure up to the ideal. You are accustomed to enjoying the experience of being alive, and however constricted your life becomes you go on enjoying it much of the time from force of habit. There are periods of black depression, but they pass; you learn by experience after a time that they will pass, and so they become less black. Where there is pain in an illness – and there was never any in mine – I doubt if it grows less burdensome with time. Continuous weakness and fatigue are bad enough. One would gladly escape them. But the kind of life they force one to lead becomes in the end as normal and natural as an active life seems to those who are active, at least for the time being. Though not entirely. There are people who become so used to an invalid's life that they find it not only livable but desirable and resent any effort to move them from it. We continue to regard this behaviour as an aberration and most invalids, however well they may be adapted to their invalidity, are still anxious to end it as soon as possible. And I don't think this is just from a general wishful thought that the grass is greener on the other side of the fence. It is, after all, natural to be active and useful. It is unnatural to be inert. Yet life, however circumscribed, is still livable; and as an experience it is not unfruitful.

An invalid is self-centred. It is often remarked and it is true. Bedridden, I was the centre of my world, not only metaphorically but in fact. There I was, in bed, fixed; and stretching from me was my world. And a very small world it was. The floor below, the ceiling above, the four walls around; a door in one wall, a window in another, and through the window a view. Through the door the world came to me and went from me. I was, or seemed to be, the object of its pilgrimage. I saw things happening through the window too, of course; yet a view to a person who can't pass through the window to join it is no part of his physical world. It was like reading books or listening to the radio, endlessly interesting, but apart. Like a private cinema screen in place of the public cinema I heard about but couldn't go to see it occupied hours of watching, wondering, seeing incredible adventures to folk whose existence I could yet not prove nor really believe in.

Two women gossiped across a gate. I couldn't hear them: sound didn't carry so far – if there was any sound, and how could I tell? I watched the drawing together, the drifting apart. The heads that went forward, the feet that went back, the swinging of the gate and the plucking of the leaves, the wagging emphatic nose and the deprecating hand. The one who wanted to get away and edged over the footpath; then remembered something and dashed back to her station. But the other wasn't so interested and leaned down to examine the growth of the daffodils.

At last when they did part, when they parted by a series of ballet exercises, two steps forward, one step back, when they departed they disappeared into their houses to prepare dinners or to dust mantelpieces, so it might be thought. But were there any dinners? Did dinners exist which were never seen by the watcher, did people eat cabbage and roast mutton behind that facade of weatherboard and lace curtains and tasselled blinds, were there any mantelpieces? When a southerly was blowing smoke in horizontal streams across a grey sky from every chimney in sight, I might infer that families were sitting around the fireplace, sitting in some manner of unimagined chair, doing what? Smoking a pipe, perhaps, listening to the radio, reading a book, drinking tea, knitting an orange sock size six, telephoning an enemy. All these things perhaps. But this was fantasy: reason, which demanded proof, had no proof at all that any of these things existed, except in thought. Was there in fact anything at all behind the weatherboard facade but an abyss of nothing?

A car appeared on the street where it came into view beyond the birch trees, and swiftly drove to that point where the street was cut off by the corner of the windowframe, passing from nowhere to nowhere, a glimpse of a shape, a fuzz of colour, its only occupant. On warm days a slower figure might come into view, an older folk out for an airing, moving with care step by step in consideration for its arthritis, holding on to fences as it passed, pausing, looking down into a flower-bed or the depths of a shrubbery, moving on, flicking a stone from the path with the point of its walking stick. And busy people walked briskly past making for somewhere they seemed to know without doubt existed, even if it didn't. And children crowded along the road, coming from school it was said; children who revealed themselves more than their parents did because they knew even less how to conceal themselves in their demeanour. Children running up the road kicking a tin, children shrieking together their twice-times table, children who said, 'I'll tell on you,' who ran their pencils along the palings of the fence opposite, who threw stones at the insulators and at the pupils of the Catholic school, who passed in a solitude of glory with pages no one but they could see holding trains made from air, who galloped along with all their cobbers who could get near shaking the reins encircling their shoulders, who read comics and the *School Journal* and told what they thought of their teachers and rounded in a mob on one of their number and beat him up and left him howling in the gutter.

I also had a paddock outside my window (we now lived in Papanui), in which there were three or four black-and-white Friesian cows, who ambled from one corner to another, walking stiffly from the hips as if they too were old ladies with sciatica. They emerged one by one from the cowshed on a frosty morning blowing white clouds of breath before them, they tugged at the hay laid out for them and stood rotating their cuds in melancholy abstraction; at four o'clock they found themselves absentmindedly assembled in a semi-circle around the cowshed waiting to be milked again by the senior boys of the Children's Home to which they belonged. On Sunday afternoons these same senior boys gathered in the loft above the cowshed and talked, poking their heads occasionally through the unglazed window, but keeping the cigarettes they were smoking out of sight. They never found another place so handy when the cows were banished from this increasingly urban neighbourhood, the cowshed demolished, a new home built where the boys had formerly played and the cow-paddock turned into a playing field. 'It's easy to see old Ma T. planned this place,' said an old boy, returning to see the new low brick building – 'windows looking out on every corner of the ground.' The gardener from Caithness stalked across the paddock towards the hawthorn hedge dividing it from the lucerne paddock. The assistant gardener laboured after him piled with rakes and shovels; the gardener's obese labrador dog, Hamish, rumbled after the assistant gardener; two or three variously coloured cats stalked after Hamish. The gardener from Caithness spied me watching from my window and waved, called something in his mezzo-soprano which I didn't catch; I nodded and waved. The foreground of my view was the yellow-green of the grass, intersected by the patterns of hedges; the middle distance was the darker green of trees, interspersed by red roofs; the far distance the mountains behind Oxford, blue or purple or white according to the season, close or far, hazy or sharp, according to the day. People who visited me admired my view, but supposed I must get tired of looking at the same scene day after day. I didn't know what they meant; the scene gave me no chance to get tired of it, it never remained precisely the same an hour at a time, certainly not for a day or a month or a year.

Visitors arrived through the door to my room, appeared like a genie from a bottle, and removed themselves back into the bottle when they left. Few of them in arriving or departing crossed the view I could see from the window. They belonged to a different world, a world that began at the door. They came nearer than the people in the view, it was less easy to disbelieve in their existence, at least while they were with me; what they became when they left was perhaps another matter. They came to the invalid as Mahomet went to the mountain, because he couldn't come to them, some of them because they wanted to, some from a sense of duty. They entertained the invalid each after his own fashion, and some without knowing it. There were, for instance, the scared, who had been hooked and had found no way of escape.

'Will you come and see Dennis for a minute,' they had been asked.

'Well, oh, er,' they had said, and then they had pulled themselves together and had allowed themselves to be propelled upstairs to perform their act of charity. They came in shaking.

'Hello,' said the invalid.

'Hello,' they said.

'Lovely day,' I said.

'Not the day to be in bed,' they said. Or,

'Not a nice day', I said, and,

'You're in the best place today,' they said. And some of them to pass the time knocked a little pattern with their knees or their knuckles on the end of the bed and sent minor earthquakes travelling up and down my spine.

'What do you do with yourself all day?' they wanted to know. 'I go mad if I'm in bed for a day.'

'Oh, I manage,' the patient assured them, exercising patience.

'I'll bring you round some Digests,' they told me, and they fled.

But there were the women (they were nearly all women – as the scared ones were nearly all men) who knew what an invalid wanted and gave it to me, who dashed in breathless from travelling in the world, collapsed into the chair, unravelled string bags from their fingers, and gave me all the news of the neighbourhood.

'Lovely day,' they said, 'the trees are beautiful in the park. I've just been to see Mrs So-and-so. Did you hear about her youngster? The teacher was telling them about the Great Wall of China, and she told them it was so *old,* and young Jim hops up and says it was built before B.B.C. wasn't it? You never know what they're going to say next. And so old Mr Dash has passed away at last. It's a sad loss but a merciful release. Ah, well, we learn life's lessons in a hard school. I won't tire you now. I have to get along and get tea. We're having sausages.' And she flew out to collect the sausages, leaving before she had tired me, leaving before there was any exhaustion to recover from, and leaving a near belief that there was a world, leaving an idea of how it was populated, and pictures to occupy the mind for days to come.

My best sort of visitor was usually more tiring than this, both because he stayed longer and because he engaged my emotions more fully. He was the kind who was in things; whose conversation took a trip through the Who's Who of all the people I'd lived alongside for years, without ever meeting. He usually had glasses and unruly hair. She, if it were a she, usually had glasses and unruly hair. He sat in the chair at the foot of my bed with his hands behind his head, his legs stretched nearly to the door; and as he talked he slipped further and further down into the chair until he was all but resting on his shoulder-blades.

He went through the Who's Who and gave me the lowdown. He took a book from the shelves beside him and weighed it in his hand.

'Now this is really good,' he said, 'this is excellent. Real downright honest everyday New Zealand. No tuis in the kowhai dell in this. Straight Pig Islanders like you'd meet in the first pub you'd go to. Of course,' he said, putting the book back in its place, 'I know old Bill well.'

'*Do* you?' I said, breathing hard for what I hoped was coming.

'Good bloke old Bill,' the visitor said, 'a real solid citizen. Of course he's an intellectual snob: he's highly educated himself and he can't understand how there can be anybody who isn't, so he can't stand the hoi polloi of course, but he's a good sort, Bill. Got married again last week. His first wife's setting up a marriage guidance clinic.'

I stored it all up. Now I was beginning to know people, now they were coming alive. 'You know who's in charge of that marriage guidance clinic?' someone else might say to me the following week, and I would say, oh yes I knew *that,* as if there could be anything happening I didn't know. And I read the real *Who's Who in New Zealand,* studied up the s's of and m's and had ready at my fingertips the ages and complicated family trees of several of our great.

And meanwhile I said to my visitor, 'And what about Such-and-such?' and my visitor told me about Such-and-such, who, it seemed, was really quite illiterate but managed to get by; and then my dragon arrived to tell the visitor it was time to leave and I lay back to recover from the visit and spent an hour watching a fly crawl across the ceiling and dreamed of the famous.

My dragon: that most necessary institution to an invalid. When he's had enough of talking he can't himself rise up and make remarks about work awaiting him at home. He has to lie and endure, and habits of good behaviour inhibit him from suggesting to the visitors that it is time they went. He may, as a voice goes on and on, press further back on to his pillows, he may yawn, his eyes may grow glassy. The kind of person he most enjoys having will be on the lookout for these symptoms and go almost too soon at a sign of them; but a remarkable number of people will remain quite oblivious to them and talk inexorably on. This is when the dragon intervenes. It is considered quite natural for an invalid's guardian to tell a visitor when to go. There is nothing impolite about this. The visitor regards it as showing a proper concern for the invalid's health. Or else as a piece of unnecessary fussing; but still, he goes. He won't realise that if there has been any warning of the visit the dragon and her ward will have fixed the exact hour at which she should intervene, and that it will have been set with much less regard for the patient's state of health than for the visitor's known capacity for talking without boring. Otherwise things would be intolerable. There is only one thing worse to an invalid than being unable to escape from a conversation when he wants to. That is when someone leaves in the middle of an argument, having had what he thinks is the last word, leaving the invalid with *his* last word unsaid.

But visitors were the casual people; they came, they entertained, they went back again to their own world. They didn't know the agitation they had caused before they came, the excitement, the thinking up of topics to talk about, the composition of bright impromptu remarks; they didn't know the satisfaction they had left when they had gone; that for days while they were going unheeding through their own business, their conversation, their looks, their attitudes, were being replayed over and over in the mind like a favourite gramophone record, and that if they called again perhaps several months afterwards they would find me ready to resume a conversation they had entirely forgotten they ever engaged in, ready to challenge opinions they didn't remember holding.

The family was there all the time: the parents; the brother and the sister who were married but turned up with their families from time to time. And the cat, who slept on the end of my bed most of the day in winter, who in summer preferred the shade, the fresh breezes and the warm earth under the delphiniums (blue) but who even then climbed the stairs every morning to pay me a brief visit before retiring outside.

The family was the daily link with the world. Meals came through the door by them, requests were sent out, shopping was done, the bed was made, mail was delivered, by them.

My father would arrive with the breakfast tray in the morning, and while I sugared and milked and ate my porridge he would sit in the chair at the foot of the bed and tell me about the meeting last night: what he said and what the enemy said, and with what arguments and manoeuvering he had won his point. He would tell me how he had accompanied a clergyman in the morning to try and make arrangements for the care of two elderly sisters, one of whom had been found having a heart attack on the sofa after her sister had poured the contents of a chamber pot over her. He would tell me how a small boy had stopped him in the street and had asked him if he was a little bit deaf and did that thing in his ear help because his grandfather was deaf and they told him he ought to have one but he said he wouldn't wear one of the damn' things. He would tell me the Dean was confined to bed with 'flu, that Sir Something thought the Minister of Finance made a very poor job of the budget speech, that the general opinion was that You know who had had a bit more than a *nervous* breakdown, but seemed to be enjoying Hanmer. He would tell me that finally he had been called from the meeting to try and pacify a woman who was about to be murdered by her husband and had found him drunk with alcohol and her with psychoanalysis.

Then the phone would ring and my mother would call up the stairs that he was wanted over at the Home straight away to deal with a boy who threatened to slap the sub-matron over the face with a dish-cloth. He would rush to find his hat, I would yell after him not to forget to get the money from me before he went to town to buy the postal note I wanted.

My mother would be up later. She would make my bed while I sat in the chair and watched the neighbours from the window. She would leave me with a bowl of water for a sponge. She would bring up the morning tea and the mail and my dinner. The door-bell would ring and I would hear a pattering. The door would shut and I would call to know who it was. She would tell me.

'What did he want?' I would call.

'He wanted your father to give him a reference,' she would reply.

'How did he come?'

'By car.'

'How does he manage to have a car?'

'Heaven knows.'

'What make of car was it?'

'I think it was red.'

And she would hunt up a book I wanted from the sitting-room bookcase, I *thought* it was in the one by the fireplace, about the third shelf down, the left-hand end, and if it wasn't she must have shifted it because that was where it was two years ago. She would find it and set it aside until she came with the afternoon tea, when she would sit for an hour and knit or read or tell me her idea of what exactly was brewing over at the Home just now, about which she was very seldom wrong although she didn't often go to see. On Tuesdays we collaborated over the *Listener* crossword.

Sometimes she went out, to shop or to the pictures, and sometimes – it depended how I felt or what time of day – I was provided with a baby-sitter. It might be the Scots gardener, who arrived with his knitting and a love story by F. J. Thwaites, and who spent much of his time listening-in on the phone, which we shared with the Home. Or it might be Miss J., with whom I had friendly, interminable, inconclusive conversations about the wickedness of Dr Malan, and the wickedness of turning food into casein, and the pleasure of playing in a percussion band, and the uselessness of labour-saving devices, and the things the leader-writers in the paper did to the King's English, and the wickedness of Dr Malan. We would argue about politics. I would accuse her of being sentimental, she would let me know she thought me a reactionary. And I would reflect that not many baby-sitters had political argument thrown in with their other duties to their charges, and that not many babies would have had such an accommodating sitter to argue with.

The other members of the family came sometimes. Children are normally shy of an adult in bed in the day-time – it isn't natural. But when they were around much of the time it came to seem natural, at least that Dennis should be in bed. My eldest niece was just reaching the age of asking questions about it; meanwhile it was quite satisfactory to have a stationary uncle who was there all of the time or at least for as long as her mother allowed her to worry him. She thought up appropriate games, for which I had to go to sleep and be wakened by her over and over, interminably. Then she sat on my bed and drew houses and my nephew sat on my bed and drew Jeeps.

On the family everything depended. I didn't lie there agonising about my dependence. It was, for the time being, the natural way of life; I had come to take it for granted, too much so perhaps, and so had they. Yet it would not have done much good to apologise every time I had to ask them to do anything. It might have eased my conscience; it would have made theirs uncomfortable. To accept what must be done for him is an invalid's necessary duty of humility; that, and refraining from asking too much, and to be content to wait for something to be brought until the bringer would be coming in any case. It isn't easy at first not to want something the moment you think of it, since to an active person the thought brings the thing, almost without his being conscious of the interposing exercise of legs and hands; but after a time the habit of patience grows. It even becomes so automatic it is no longer a virtue but merely one more part of a way of living.

A life lived in this little boxed-up universe which differed so from the world other people lived in, not only in its space but in its time. Time in that room was an elementary thing which travelled quietly in even distances marked off by meals and bedmaking and by the radio programmes. And as a visitor enlarged for a time the dimensions of space he was also interrupting the progress of time – and I missed my favourite radio serial perhaps. I realised for a moment that time didn't always run to my command alone. Other owners of time demanded its service. But my time soon recovered its own pace, and for long stretches it might stop altogether while I watched the fly on the ceiling or the children on the street or the women over the fence or the shifting colours on the mountains to the west. The invalid in these days is one of the few remaining exponents of the contemplative life.

A life of contemplation – and of waiting.

Three

It was just before Christmas, 1949, that my father was arranging to go into hospital early the following year to have a hernia operation. The superintendent of the Christchurch hospital was an acquaintance of his, and my father dropped into his office one day to discuss the arrangements, and in passing mentioned me. Well, apparently in passing. The superintendent pricked up his ears and said I should also enter the hospital for up-to-date tests to decide whether there would be any point in sending me to Green Lane. The cardio-surgical unit there, he said, liked to see all congenital heart cases even if there was only the faintest chance that they might be helped.

From that time the waiting became fixed on a particular point; and all through that summer time seemed to have slowed down, to have stopped altogether. On Christmas day I went out for a longer time than I had done for two or three years, to the home of my niece's other grandparents, where I sat with my feet up on the couch – except when a family photograph was taken, and I sat upright like a human being – on the wide, white-painted veranda, watching relatives and in-laws play tennis on the lawn, receiving presents from the tree, watching excited children opening their presents. Every now and then when exhaustion threatened I disappeared into a bedroom and lay down for a while before joining the party again. In another room my niece's great-grandmother lay dying. 'Bodies in every room' said an in-law, barging into mine and out again. After two hours I'd had enough and was taken home, tired out but thinking it had been worth it.

We had more visitors than usual during January to keep me occupied; we also had my father's operation to keep my mind from dwelling exclusively on the possibility of having one of my own; and still the days refused to move. But they must have done, eventually, because I did go into hospital. My father by that time was convalescing in Auckland; my mother couldn't drive; the Scots gardener could but wouldn't because every person he had driven to hospital had died there. So I went in a taxi, and stayed twelve days: twelve days occupied by talking to the other patients, and lying under the blankets so that I needn't, stitching a piece of tapestry supplied by the occupational therapist, which later lay for several years unfinished in a drawer at home until I gave it away – not that I didn't want to do it, but I hadn't time; sitting for short periods on the balcony and watching white-shorted nurses and doctors playing tennis on the courts below, patients strolling along the gravel walks in their dressing-gowns, nurses and sisters in their long starched uniforms which Christchurch alone of all the New Zealand hospitals still clung to; mother ducks exercising their families from the Avon on the lawns under the incomparable trees; not listening to the radio which descended vague and crackling from the ceilings of each of the small rooms in Ward 12, splattering Empire Games on unheeding heads; being woken up one night by an earthquake. It was a wider world in itself, hard to get used to and tiring, but exciting.

And, infrequently and almost incidentally, examinations by doctors, lettings of blood for analysis, giving of urine, an electro-cardiograph test from a machine vastly different from the first I had known, though the operator assured me proudly that an even better one was arriving at Lyttelton the following week. Finally I was raced in a chair along corridors to have X-ray photographs taken and a screening. The screening was conducted by a pleasant young man wearing horn-rimmed spectacles and a rubber apron, who was descended, I discovered, from one of the city's best-known statues.

I stood behind the screen and was fed with spoonfuls of barium while the radiologist watched my insides moving before him. When I grew tired – I couldn't stand for more than a minute or two at a time – I sat to recover my breath in the wheelchair while he talked to me of television, which, no doubt because he was in the same line of business, he evidently thought would be a good thing. And because it was to me the comfortable way of sitting and was a habit of mine, I drew my feet up on to the seat of the wheelchair, and squatted. This interested him a lot, for a reason I could not then fathom; but I later discovered that this squatting, which my family had always taken to be one of my own funny little ways, is an infallible symptom of the one genuine original blue-baby. Whether this gave him an idea what to look for or whether he had spotted it already I don't know, but when my mother came to the hospital two days later, having been assured on her previous visits that mine was not a case which could be helped by surgery, she was now told there was a remote chance of an operation and that I should be sent to Auckland. My particulars would be sent to Green Lane; meanwhile I should return home and wait for their summons. My mother was then sent into the ward to tell me while we waited for the taxi to take us home; and when I was wheeled from the ward by one of the nicest of the nurses, the excitement had made me a blue enough blue-baby to convince the most sceptical doctor of my true identity.

I don't think I once doubted from that moment it would happen in the end. And everybody said, they may *say* it's only a remote possibility, but that's medical caution. They're protecting you from disappointment in case nothing can be done, but they wouldn't be sending you that distance if they didn't think there was a good chance. I believed them. We began suddenly to hear of other cases, and to be astonished at the number there were. We heard most often of a boy at Christ's College who had been successfully operated on. It seemed that everybody to whom we mentioned my coming trip to Auckland knew about him, and they all described his great improvement. When I told the barber, who came to cut my hair, while I sat on the end of my bed and he dodged among the other furniture in my tiny room to get behind my right ear, that I was going to Green Lane, he said, 'Like young T.' The lawyer who came to help me make my will said, 'Like young T.' The wife of one of the masters at the school said, 'Like young T.' It was a refrain that seemed to come trippingly off everyone's tongue. My father also heard about young T. from the former Minister of Health. It was he she had seen being carved up, and as she was unable to stay to the end of the long job she had left with an unsatisfied curiosity to know what they had done with the ribs they had laid aside in a dish.

We waited, expecting to hear any moment from Green Lane. There was no word. They were putting through blue-babies in batches and still they came. In April the Christchurch doctors suggested my mother and I should force their hand by appearing in Auckland anyway: we could stay with my aunt who had a couple of beds to spare on the North Shore, and there make sure we were not out of sight out of mind. They saw no reason why I should not fly, so our seats were booked, our friends and relations gathered to say good-bye, my father had permission to drive the car on to the tarmac to the door of the plane, and I was in it, we were flying. I was dozing with my mother's fur coat as a pillow to absorb some of the vibration, glancing at the scene below and shutting my eyes again and I was not conscious of any more discomfort than could be fully accounted for by being out of my bed longer than I had been for years, by the excitement, and by the number of bumps near the end of the journey. But later doctors, when all was known, were horrified that I should have flown at all without extra oxygen.

My aunt's doctor had arranged for an ambulance to meet the plane at Whenuapai. The driver was unsure of the state of the road around the head of the harbour and decided to drive into town and to cross the harbour by the vehicular ferry. It was growing dark and the windows of the ambulance were frosted: I saw little of the journey, only odd glimpses through the curtain dividing the back of the van from the front seat.

An ambulance need not wait in the queue for the ferry at Auckland. Like a hearse, with which we occasionally shared the privilege in the next few weeks, it drives straight on. What is more, in an emergency the driver can order the ferry to leave immediately, without waiting for the scheduled time. The driver evidently considered this an emergency and ordered the ferry away with scarcely any cars on board. The crew were just about to have a cup of tea and were not pleased. We arrived at Bayswater; I went to bed and had sufficient strength for an egg flip. My mother and my aunt no doubt talked. I stayed quiet.

My mother rang the hospital in a day or two and was given an appointment to see the Superintendent. She woke on the morning with an eye swollen to an enormous size. Mosquitoes, who in Auckland are large and aggressive and hungry for new blood, had skilfully planted a ring of bites right around it. She looked as if she had been in a fight; she was sure it would ruin my chances of a cure, that no self-respecting Medical Superintendent would pay attention to anyone so disreputable. But she applied lotions vigorously until it was time to go, pulled her hat well down over the eye, and risked it. He listened to her story and gave me an appointment to see the cardiosurgical clinic three weeks hence.

Meanwhile I was settled in my room in Bayswater. I had a glimpse from my window of one of the quiet inlets of the Waitemata harbour, which became one large sheet of sand at low tide. The dinghies moored under the cliff spent half their time on dry land half a mile from any water, and the other half floating placidly in the sea. There were houses among the pohutukawas up the cliff, and a gasometer showed above them. In the garden was a lemon tree, which a tui visited every day. For short periods I sat on the window-seat in the living-room, looking across the full width of the harbour to the city, watching the ferries float across on a course so straight and steady they might have been on rails, watching the occasional big ship arriving or leaving, and the smaller craft, the police and harbour board and navy launches and the private yachts, skimming to and fro.

I had a wireless by my bed belonging to another aunt who was then in Ireland. It had a silver plate attached to it recording that it had been presented to her on her retirement by the boarders of the school of which she had been Lady Principal. The plate was live: it tingled when you touched it. This was subtle of the boarders but it had not yet worked and I kept my fingers away from it. I had more magazines than I could cope with (I couldn't settle to books), and most days some visitor would be popping in for a few minutes, a friend of my aunt's or of ours.

To encourage the time to go more quickly I did something quite new: I learned to play a tin whistle. It was the nearest thing to a musical instrument I had ever tackled; it was bought for me by the person in the neighbouring flat, who worked in one of the big music stores. It was not tin, it wasn't even a tin whistle officially; it was made of plastic, red white and blue, and the leaflet which accompanied it called it a flageolet. From this leaflet I played myself into a stupor the first night and proudly produced before I went to sleep a tune which I recognised as *The Church's One Foundation*, though no one else did. I tootled myself through one of the *Dominion Song Books*, using mainly the sol fa printed beneath the notes, and learned to play *Oh Hush Thee My Baby*, *The Mermaid,* and several other pieces well enough to be recognised by other people as well as myself, though I had to take three times as many breaths as were provided for in the music. The tenant in the other flat and his wife followed sympathetically the progress of the pipings that penetrated the sound-proofed walls between, and the husband retaliated in kind with selections from *Oklahoma* and Handel's *Largo* on the piano. I believe my red white and blue plastic flageolet saved my life at that time, which might otherwise have been overcome by the strain of waiting, of wondering.

Four

I had two appointments, for a Thursday morning and for the following Tuesday morning. Thursday-Tuesday, Thursday-Tuesday: it was a routine with which I was to become familiar. Tests were done on the Thursday and the results considered by the Clinic on the following Tuesday. The Thursday appointment was for 8.15, and to be sure of getting there in time meant an early start. We went by ambulance again, partly for its priority on the ferry, for which queues of cars sometimes waited for more than an hour. As we drove through to Devonport, and from Mechanic's Bay to Green Lane on the other side, I saw as much as I could of the scenery through the curtain, and over the top of the window, which was lowered a little; though in going through busy places like Newmarket where the traffic lights held us up at every intersection, the driver kept the curtain pulled tight across, not to prevent me seeing but to save me from curious eyes. 'People', he said, 'will go to any length to look inside an ambulance.' I should certainly have disappointed anyone wanting a sensation – no blood, no deformities, no premature babies. It was a pity they were not allowed the disappointment.

Between the two landward parts of the journey there was time to see the harbour; first of all on the wharf at Devonport where we had to wait, in spite of the priority, for the ferry to arrive with the replacement ambulance which was always sent across when the North Shore ambulance had to cross to town. As we waited I could look along the grey-green water to the islands misty in the distance. The trip over the harbour was by far the smoothest part of the journey. We rose and fell gently, we did not joggle or bump. Ambulance travel on land was not the smoothest I had tried, especially in ambulances from the North Shore. The latest ambulances were built on the chassis of Humber and Mercury cars, but the town headquarters of the brigade did not allow these to cross the harbour. The driver who told me this implied jealousy; but I suppose they were afraid the salt spray might sully their new shine, or that they might be liable to dents and scratches boarding the ferry. So I travelled on the pre-war Bedford truck chassis, which were serviceable but not luxuriously sprung. There was also, I was told, one ambulance built on to an ageing Rolls-Royce, but I never had the distinction of travelling in this, because of its extreme length and unmanoeuvrability. As we floated across the driver agitated my mother's bad-travelling stomach with tales of sailing in the yacht race from Auckland to Sydney, but she bore it without flinching.

When we arrived at Green Lane he backed in close to the entrance, so that I had no chance to admire the imposing six-storey face of the main block, of which there is a picture in *Everyman's Encyclopaedia*, illustrating 'a splendid example of the modern conception of a hospital'. ('I can think of some better ones,' an architectural friend said, when I mentioned this fact to him.) The driver found a chair, I was wheeled up a ramp to the panelled, low-ceilinged foyer, into a lift, up two floors, and deposited in a corridor outside a door marked *Cardio-Surgical Clinic.* We sat and watched nurses in white overalls, with their hair tucked into white kerchiefs, dashing up and down with plates of porridge and bedpans. The Sister in charge of the Clinic appeared at the end of the corridor, brisk and poised, smiling as if she was pleased to see us, her eyes twinkling. She took my particulars and then returned me downstairs to the X-ray department in the charge of one of the X-ray orderlies. There were two of them: one tall, black-haired, spectacled, smiling; the other grey-haired, slightly stooped, dour; and they spent their time shuttling up and down from wards to X-ray, waving pieces of paper describing their charges. The X-ray department was housed in an ancient yellow-brick outhouse dating from the time when this was the Costley Home for Incurables, before it had begun its progression through the Epsom Infirmary to the Green Lane Hospital. The new main block, which had completed the transformation, though no doubt it had been a good deal more costly than the Costley Home, had also been designed for incurables, or as they call them nowadays more politely, geriatrics, and had no provision for X-rays, laboratories, operating theatres and other frills, which had to be improvised when it was turned into an acute hospital during the war. Even the Cardio-Surgical Clinic occupied what should have been the patients' lounge. All this I learned later from the barber, who had worked in the hospital through all its metamorphoses.

I was shown into a cubicle, told to remove my upper clothing and replace it with a fluffy, enveloping cotton nightgown. Then I waited. Others who had waited before me had scratched their initials in the plaster; one had written, 'HURRY UP.' The bench was narrow and I had difficulty keeping myself upright on it, and finally squatted on the floor. The X-ray Sister came past. 'Ah, squatting,' she said, and no doubt kept it in her head for future reference.

At last I was stood against a wall and told to hold my breath, there was the usual whirr while I was riddled with rays, and I was put back into the cubicle to wait while the films were developed; then there was a screening by an enormously tall radiologist who had to fold himself more than a human being normally can, to get himself to the right level. I was delivered back to the Clinic and laid aside by the Sister on a bed in one of the rooms of the ward until she was ready for me, separated by a screen from the rest of the roomful of pale prone old men with indigestion.

When the Sister was ready for me once more she took me to the bed in the Clinic, where she removed blood from an arm and capped it in a glass tube; then prodded my chest in several places with ink pencil, shaved any hairs from the way, anointed the spots with a conducting ointment, affixed suction cups, strapped electrodes to the wrists and ankles, each attached by a differently coloured flex to the bright new cream-enamel electrocardiograph machine, pulled switches and recorded my electric currents, chatting pleasantly. 'Are you English?' she wanted to know, 'or just Christchurch?'

The walls were attractively hung with nursery pictures to entertain us blue-babies; the view, when I was upright enough to see it, looked up to the three trees and mirror topped obelisk on One Tree Hill, and down to a large vegetable garden which I supposed must belong to the hospital; and immediately below to the unprepossessing rows of Tb shelters, furnace houses and storehouses.

The Sister then handed me over, surprisingly, to a vocational guidance officer, who led me to a tiny room where, sitting among buckets and boilers and ladders and blankets, I arranged coloured strips of cardboard into required patterns, solved elementary jigsaws, arranged the separate pictures of Soglow cartoons into the order which told a story, repeated lists of figures backwards, and answered such general knowledge posers as, 'Where is London?' After that I was allowed to go home until the following Tuesday.

As I was being loaded into the ambulance the X-ray Sister came by. I did not hear her say to my mother:

'You've left it a bit late to bring him, haven't you?'

On the Tuesday it was the ambulance again, up to the Clinic again, down to X-ray for another screening, where I walked into the darkness to be confronted not by one radiologist but by a whole circle of ghostly figures who watched while the radiologist discoursed about my insides and pointed out the salient features – with frequent pauses to let me squat when I needed to – in language which was mostly, and no doubt intentionally, too technical for me to understand, except for an occasional phrase like, 'See what a beautifully clear aorta.'

Back at the Clinic I was listened to by a doctor, and my mother and I were closely questioned on every point of ancestry, past history from conception onwards and present behaviour, and he dictated the answers, suitably translated, to a stenographer. That finished, I was left laid out ready for the queue of the same figures, no longer ghostly, I had seen at the screening; they ran me over with their stethoscopes in strict order of precedence, beginning with the part-time specialists and surgeons, through the Medical Superintendent, the registrars and house surgeons, down to the sixth-year students. Some of them said 'Hello' as they arrived, some of them said 'Ah' or 'Right' or 'Thank you' as they left. Two of the students were girls; they waited their turn respectfully to the last.

My mother and I were then removed along the corridor out of earshot while the doctors talked me over. Dinner had long ago been served in the ward, the medicine trolley was trundled past, some of the nurses were coming back from their dinners, to replace their blue uniforms with white overalls and prepare the patients for visitors, the second shift were rushing off, throwing their capes over their shoulders, to eat in their turn. Still the doctors talked, still we waited to hear whether they were going to operate or not. I drooped on the chair from the effort to keep alert, but unable to relax until they gave their verdict.

The Superintendent, who had the not always happy task of acting as spokesman for the Clinic, came out into the corridor, very kind, very friendly. They could give no verdict yet, he said; there were more tests they would like to do, for which I would be admitted to the hospital. We would hear from them when I was to go in.

We returned to Bayswater: back to the view, to the flageolet, to the neighbours dropping in, for another long fortnight; until the ambulance was called for the second-to-last time, and I was taken back to Green Lane. They wheeled me into the main block, up a few floors in the lift. Nurses looked at me. They brought other nurses to look at me. There was a pause while I sat in my chair and patients made polite remarks; and then I was wheeled to another part of the hospital altogether. It turned out later that Ward 3, having been warned to expect a blue-baby, had prepared for a child, and had no place to put a 24-year-old.

Ward 18, to which I was now admitted, was a men's medical ward. It was on the first floor of one of the older blocks of the hospital, and was *not* shown in *Everyman's Encyclopaedia.* There was no lift and I had to be carried up the lofty flight of stairs by two orderlies, who held me nearly upside-down in a complicated canvas arrangement. I was put into bed, and soon afterwards a patient came along with a trolley, asked me how many slices of bread I wanted with my tea, and left them on a plate with a blob of butter, another of jam, and a knife. It seemed a bit early for tea – although it was the end of May the sun still shone brightly into the ward – but I knew hospitals kept early hours and I buttered and jammed and started to eat.

The patient, returning to the kitchen with his trolley, raised his eyebrows as he passed. 'Are you hungry?' he said. The other patients knew, but I did not, that he liked to get his part of the job done early and that the rest of the tea would not arrive for another hour. I was obviously in a world where it did not do to take anything for granted.

I was in Ward 18 for a month. It was a long ward containing thirty beds; and thirty people (not to mention the nurses and doctors) was a good many more than I had been among for many years. The nurses had the pleasant habit of introducing a new patient to his neighbours on either side; but even without the introductions everyone soon knew each other pretty intimately. The impression I had of the looks of each of them as I sat in my bed that first sunny afternoon was so filled out and modified by the evidence of their behaviour which accumulated day by day that it was almost impossible to recall after that time how they had looked at first.

None of the patients near me was desperately ill. They were either recovering, or, like me, were having tests from which the doctors would decide their future action. We were at the further end of the ward from the Sister's office. When patients began to move space by space nearer to her we knew things were pretty bad. When they arrived against the very end wall they had only two alternatives; either they reversed direction and began travelling again towards us; or screens were put up, orderlies tramped from the bed to the door, with only their feet showing beneath the screens; the bedclothes were removed and the bed thoroughly scrubbed before someone else came to occupy it. But up our way we were comparatively lively, and the main occupation of the patients around me was keeping themselves occupied. They read; but not very much, and seldom anything more solid than a Digest; they organised sweeps on the races; they listened to the radios which were installed while I was there – little pillow-speakers, audible only about two or three inches from the ear, so that if I had mine turned off I could not hear any other but could see the faces around me change expression simultaneously. Some of them did occupational therapy; one made model aeroplanes and sent them flying along the ward when the Sister wasn't looking. Those who were up wandered from bed to bed gathering an anthology of symptoms and life stories or gazed out of the window at the traffic passing along Green Lane – which is not a lane at all but a main thoroughfare for that part of Auckland, and is labelled on at least one signpost *Green Lane Road.* I speculated whether there had once been a green lane along the foot of One Tree Hill, or whether the lane had belonged to a Mr Green. I don't yet know. Nor did I get on much better trying to identify the three other volcanic humps which arose in the horizon on my side of the ward. I asked Aucklanders bred and born, and each of them contradicted all the others. It wasn't until I was able to get hold of a map that I could identify them as being, from left to right, Mounts Eden, St John and Hobson. We could also watch trotters exercising around the course at Alexandra Park across the road; but there was no meeting while I was there. And on Saturdays up patients gathered in the day-room to watch minor-grade Rugby on the Showgrounds.

They were all, like me, living in a different world from their own, although for most of them it was a narrower, not a wider world; but they brought with them hints of their various backgrounds and acted as encased specimens of a world I hoped to enter before long. Hints, indeed, of a greater variety of lives than I was ever likely to enter, especially as this hospital was in the most cosmopolitan of our cities.

In a bed against the opposite wall from mine was a sixteen-year-old Maori boy. He had come from a remote East Coast district to one of the Maori colleges near Auckland and had only been there a short time – not long enough to have seen Auckland itself – when he caught rheumatic fever, which had damaged his heart. He was a lively youngster, immensely curious about everything around him, firing off rapid questions in an English very different from the accent used by the more sophisticated Maoris who lived nearer the city, receiving the answers with delighted wonder. He made felt Donald Ducks for the occupational therapist, read comics, threw paper darts, drew large pictures of cowboys; and towards the end of the time I was there began doing school lessons. The other patients had him teach them rude words in Maori. He was most of the time the most cheerful character in the ward. But he had few visitors. His headmaster came occasionally, and his mother spent a weekend in Auckland, a plump comfortable person; but the journey from home was so long she couldn't repeat it often; and sometimes, when she had just gone, or when the doctors told him he must stay in hospital at least another six months, he burrowed under the bedclothes and wept.

There was a young Samoan, a Mormon, who arrived wearing a double-breasted grey suit of American cut and a boisterous tie, and kept religious literature along with the comics in his locker. There was a round-faced Indian, older than these, who also had rheumatic fever. He kept a shop outside, and was also a bookmaker, with a large and distinguished clientele, so he told me, mentioning some of the names to establish his bona fides. He assured me the Totalisator Agency Board, which was then just in the planning stage, was going to be the end of the bookies; but meanwhile his wife was carrying on in his absence and arrived every weekend with a pile of cheques for him to sign, and would come shyly over to borrow my fountain-pen, a tiny, beautiful woman, smartly dressed in European style, with two tiny, beautiful, children. He also obliged patients in the ward, several of whom were shocked to find how I had been wasting my years in bed, ideally placed as I was to go into business. They begged me to mend my ways as soon as I got home and make something worthwhile of my life. The Indian bookmaker talked politics, too; and one day he discussed Robert Emmet with me.

'The English hanged him,' he said, 'just because he wanted his country to be free. The English hanged five hundred Irishmen, because they wanted to be free.'

'The pity of it is,' said a loud voice from a body prostrated with pneumonia in the next bed, which had scarcely had the energy to say a word for days, 'that they didn't hang five thousand of them.'

This old man came from Belfast. He was very tall, very lean, and might almost have been the twin of my grandfather, who came from Derry. As he recovered from his illness he was ordered to be up for part of the day for the health of his lungs, and joined the other convalescent patients in the day-room at the end of the ward; but before he could trust himself out of bed he dressed himself fully from head to toe: shirt, waistcoat, jacket, trousers, hat, shoes. And as far as I could see he kept most of them on when he returned to bed afterwards.

Another Indian, a young man with a pleasant face and a persistent pleurisy which got neither worse nor better during the month I was in the ward, never joined in the general talk, and seldom spoke at all except to his immediate neighbour. He told him one Sunday afternoon he had just had forty visitors. The news passed around the ward; none of the rest of us had been aware of it. They had gathered around his bed four or five at a time and had changed places almost imperceptibly, gliding in and out of the ward, the men dressed in sports coats and slacks, the women in saris.

A Jugoslav dairy farmer from near Kaukapakapa – a place whose existence I had never really believed in – was beside me for a time. He reminisced in an English still thick with echoes of his native Herzegovina about his first few years in New Zealand, when he and his brother had worked on the construction of the railway to Tauranga; and compared it with his present prosperity and the fine education he was giving his children, who were growing into good New Zealanders. But for the moment he was anxious about their future. He had come into hospital because of a persistent indigestion he expected to learn was cancer. Nothing of the sort was found and he returned happily to Kaukapakapa.

There was a Scotsman – the man who had brought me the slices of bread that first afternoon. He had worked for years on the Auckland tramways, and now had a spot on the lung for which he had been threatened with an operation, but which he was reducing without surgery by methodically working at the exercises he was told to do, lying on his bed with a strap around his chest, pulling it tight, and then pushing it out. In between times he was almost another nurse, fetching pans and bottles, serving drinks, slicing bread. He was often away on one of these errands when his physiotherapist called on him, and while she waited she did handsprings on the end of his bed, a display of surplus energy I thought a little callous.

There was a petty officer from the navy who said he was a New Zealander but spoke like a Yorkshireman, who was recovering from a coronary thrombosis, and who was the bookmaker's best client in the ward, but was facing up to a life outside with no race-meetings, because they would be too exciting. The doctor removed from his locker one morning a copy of *Life* with a very innocuous bathing beauty on the cover. Also too exciting. There was an elderly deaf convalescent, originally from Lancashire, who walked from bed to bed to have a chat and stood intimately close, breathing on you, to catch what you said, and denounced the extravagance of installing radios in the ward; and an Afrikaans seaman and an Australian butcher; and even a few New Zealanders.

But if we were a comparatively lively lot we were hardly as lively as the nurses who kept us in order; dozens of nurses, fat jolly girls, angular severe girls, round smooth sweet girls, slender serene girls, rowdy girls, scared girls just graduated from the preliminary school. Quite unsubdued by any worry about the problem of human suffering they kept the patients from suffering more, not only by looking after them, but by their own constant reminder of health and spirits: racing up and down the ward carrying meals and toiletries, making beds, rubbing backs, joking and chiding. And the Sister, too, who was middle-aged, well-groomed, round-limbed, sparkling, occasionally explosive (but more often at her superiors than at her inferiors), had everyone in a good humour after her tours around the beds. And there were the night supervising sisters, and the hierarchy of matrons in white linen uniforms, flowing veils and red capes, who moved quietly from bed to bed every morning. 'And how are you this morning?' a sweet smile, a move on to the next bed; but with their eyes open all the time and a little notebook in which they jotted down matters to be referred to the right quarters. 'She has eyes in her *shoes*,' said a junior, rubbing my back with methylated spirits, 'that's the only way she could have seen there was dust under the bottle-shelf in the lavatory.' The next junior to rub my back, when I referred this opinion to her for comment said, 'Oh she's a dear, really; but you have to watch out when the other one's around.'

The house physicians made an occasional appearance in the ward, looking for blood or taking particulars from a new patient or draining a lung; but the real visitations by the doctors happened every Tuesday, Thursday and Saturday mornings, when the Senior Physician, the Junior Physician, the Medical Registrar, the House Physician, half-a-dozen students and the Sister began a slow processional progress at the far end of the ward, passing from bed to bed accompanied by a trolley draped with charts – or rather with fat files of documents, still called charts from the days when medical records were less complex. The party grew larger, more ominous to the eye, as it approached nearer, like a thunder-cloud looming over the brow of a hill and taking its time about coming nearer. They never had any decisions to make about me; they left that until they and their colleagues sat as the Clinic in the other block; but they did a token listen to my chest, flicked over the chart, and ran through the latest theories about my condition for the benefit of the students. I always tried to have a few interesting magazines for them to flick through as they stood around my bed. They seemed grateful for them.

Although there were many more people in this life than in the life I had been leading it wasn't yet the life of the world. It was a highly organised society in which the different orders – including the domestic staff, who were in the ward but not quite of it – knew their station in life and the duties attached to it, and performed them and kept their station so faithfully that it was almost impossible to picture the nurses out of uniform catching a tram or courting in the park, or the patients out of their pyjamas mowing the lawn on Sunday or turning up at work on Monday. It was a noisy life at times, and that meant to me it was a tiring one; but I liked to think I was beginning to live. I also noticed a few of the difficulties of beginning to live. For one thing, after living for years with rather more books than people, I found I had to forget about half my vocabulary if I wanted to be understood; and even so the patients called me Professor, and wanted to know if I was a school teacher.

Five

Underneath the public life of the ward the private fears for the most part kept themselves hidden within each person; except when pain or fear overcame consciousness, which released its grip and a man screamed; screamed until he was hurried away to a private room and injected with sedatives, while the other patients looked at each other restlessly, wishing it wouldn't happen. It was too close to their own burden.

I was back into my Thursday-Tuesday routine. On the first Thursday I was given an angiocardiogram. This test counted as a minor operation: the preliminaries were the same and I had to sign a form permitting the hospital to take whatever steps they thought necessary to my recovery; and that one signature lasted through all the things they did to me until I left the hospital. I was taken to the X-ray department and put on a trolley. The radiologist, the surgical registrar and the X-ray sister were gathered around (though I couldn't see them well because my glasses had been removed) exchanging good-natured abuse over my body while they inserted a drip into the crook of my elbow, taking occasional notice of my presence and – having read my documents – addressing me affectionately as Richard. I hadn't the energy under the circumstances to explain to them that although Richard was officially my first name it was not the one I used, and anyway it didn't worry me what they chose to call me, so I remained Richard from that time on to those members of the hospital staff who were not so formal as to call me Mr McEldowney.

I had been given a local anaesthetic in the arm, which deadened the nerves of pain, but not – or not entirely – those of feeling, so that I could still feel their knives scratching into a vein: a point which, like the whole procedure, I found interesting but not enjoyable. I did not like having my flesh poked and prodded and opened up, and I was scared stiff throughout. My heart pounded along like an express train, and I expected them to say if I couldn't stop it doing that they wouldn't go on, and leave me in disgrace; but they took no *apparent* notice of it, and went straight ahead. They wheeled me into the screening room, transferred me on to the machine, which was now lying flat like a table, injected a radio-opaque dye into the drip, and photographed its course through the circulation, banging plates in and out of the table at tremendous speed for the few seconds the dye took to complete the circuit; and then it was over, except for the slightly inconvenient reaction which the dye produced on the patient: a torrid, searing heat, burning from the inside to the out, like one ferocious blush for all the sins I was ever guilty of. This didn't last long, but long enough. I was turned on my side, which helped it go more quickly, and was then gently sick into a basin.

It took me a day or so to recover from that; and then the Tuesday arrived. Before the Clinic sat (the word, incidentally, applied both to the place and to the doctors who assembled there) I was given another test, a small one, and quite entertaining. I held a stopwatch in my hand while sugar was injected into a vein. I started the watch when it went in and stopped it when I tasted sweetness on my tongue. This gave the time the circulation took to travel from the arm to the mouth. Then ether was injected and I had to stop the watch when I could smell it on my breath. This was the time from the arm to the lung. I forget what the times were; I thought they were quick, but they were evidently a little retarded in fact. Then I waited for the Clinic's verdict. It was delivered to my mother, who had permission to come over to the ward before the visiting hour to tell me. But it was still no verdict. The tests so far were inconclusive: there was still another to be done, on the next Thursday.

This was a catheterisation of the heart. They prepared me as they had done the week before; but this time when I was on the X-ray table a thin flexible metal catheter was inserted into a vein (using the other elbow this time, so I was left with two sore arms) and sent exploring into the heart. The radiologist, sitting somewhere above, watched its progress on the screen, photographs were taken with the same banging of plates in and out of the table beneath, the catheter took blood pressures in all the cavities it was sent into, and samples of blood were drawn out. It was a much more leisurely performance than the last one and much less unpleasant for the patient. I could feel nothing of what was going on inside me. I could hear the voices around me in the darkness – more voices than there had been before – and feel a finger on my pulse, belonging to the consulting cardiologist who was titular head of the Clinic. I was much less affected by it. I had been given a sedative this time; it had not put me to sleep during the test, but it did when I came back to the ward, beautifully, irresponsibly. I woke up, found my mother sitting by me, and went to sleep again. I woke up and knocked my glasses to the floor and slept again before I could ask anyone to pick them up. I woke up, found I was without my glasses, couldn't remember what had happened to them, and had a nurse searching through my locker. It was a happy time. I wished I could stay that way until the Tuesday, when I should hear whether there was any verdict yet. But I soon woke up.

On that Tuesday afternoon, after I had been turned around watching the main block through the window by my bed for hours,

I at last saw my mother walking across towards the ward. She had a droop about her which did not look happy, and I concluded they had either not given a verdict or they had decided they could do nothing for me. But when she arrived upstairs I found I was wrong. They had decided to operate.

I found it harder to believe they had decided than I had found it to believe they would decide. Plans for the future I had not allowed myself to dwell on now began to surge up into consciousness. It did still seem a little odd to me that although my mother joined with my excitement she did not *look* as happy as she sounded or as I felt. Yet of course she was tired after the strain of waiting. I didn't know then she hadn't told me all the Superintendent had told her. They were going to operate, he told her, because they had no option. The constriction in the pulmonary artery was very severe; there was very little blood getting through to the lungs; and if nothing was done I could live only a very short time. He was kindly but grave, and she thought he did not seem very hopeful. We later learned, when it was safe to reveal it, that they were all even less hopeful than he had implied.

I knew nothing of all this. I did know that I had been discovered to be an orthodox blue-baby (I would have picked this from the conversation of the doctors around me, even if I had not been told); and I knew enough to know that a blue-baby of 24 was an anachronism, that I could not have any expectation of life, and that there was no other option than to accept an operation. But that was not the reason why it never entered my head to refuse an operation. What I was looking forward to was not just staying alive as I had been staying alive, but to getting out of bed and really living. And I was quite certain it was going to happen: too certain to notice if anyone around me might be having doubts. Not that they intended I should notice. If I was blind it was their business to keep me blind. Nurses, sisters and doctors beamed, said they were thrilled, told me about their successful cases, talked of the things I would be able to do afterwards. Members of the family wrote cheerful letters. Patients told me Green Lane had one of the best surgeons in New Zealand – which I already knew, although I had not yet met him. He had been on holiday in Australia at the time I was appearing in person before the Clinic.

I still had a fortnight to make plans about the future, to grow nervous about the event which stood before me and the future, when I should certainly be poked and prodded to a degree I had not yet experienced, whatever else might happen. I occupied my time with the life in the ward, with sewing a pink leather slipper, with catching a cold. This last set off one of the Sister's amiable explosions. She said if she had her way visitors would all wear face-masks before they were allowed in the door, and why they didn't stay away from a hospital when they knew they had a cold she couldn't fathom. I pointed out that I had caught it from a patient in the next bed, who had been and gone and left it behind him. 'The blighter!' she said, and she subsided – until she caught it herself.... So she was off duty the day Mr R., the surgeon, arrived to see me. He was very tall, very broad, and was escorted into the ward by the Surgical Registrar like a cruiser attended by a destroyer. He spoke mildly, listened in, asked a few questions, consulted my records.

'You realise we may not be able to do anything for you?' he said. 'You may wake up and find we have not been able to give any relief.'

I said I did, and I did, intellectually; but I was more impressed by his calm unworried bearing than by his words. I felt sure that if anyone could work the miracle, this man could.

'You won't mind being moved to a surgical ward?' he said. 'We'd like to get you accustomed to the oxygen tent beforehand.' And he moved off with his escort. When the visitors for that day were also gone I was moved to the main block, trying before I went with a nurse's help to reduce a month's accumulation of rubbish in my locker sufficiently to make a reasonable pillow-case load to be carried with me. I was carried down the stairs as I had been carried up, and as every patient who could not walk had been carried up, every bed, all the bedding, every meal. The orderlies wanted to know what I was going for. 'Well, there's no better surgeon in New Zealand,' one of them said. 'Nor in Australia,' the other said. They spoke with proprietry pride. They put me on a wheeled stretcher, wrapped me in rubber sheeting because it was raining, and wheeled the load the short distance between the blocks.

I was put in a two-bed room without another occupant and was the next day kept as busy as if I were preparing for a journey. The Sister came in with enormous jugs of fruit juice with glucose which she told me to drink. I had been kept in bed in the medical ward but was now told the surgeon liked his patients to have been active the day before an operation and I trotted to and from the lavatory and when I met the Matron as she was mounting the stairs to the next floor, squatted to talk to her. The physiotherapist came to teach me breathing exercises which I must begin the moment I woke from the anaesthetic. With the blue-babies who were babies, she told me, she had to adopt stratagems, pressing a toy cat to its side and saying, 'push pussy in, push pussy out.' 'It must be easier not to have to do that,' I said. 'Yes,' she said; 'on the other hand I can't lift you up and toss you on to your stomach.'

She gave me a trial run in the oxygen tent. A transparent plastic hood, much the shape of the cab of a truck, came down over my head and shoulders and tucked into the bedclothes. Dials were adjusted on the big oxygen cylinders beside the bed. I could still see and hear.

'You don't seem to mind it,' said the physiotherapist.

I certainly didn't. I was luxuriating in the easy breathing inside this plastic bag.

'There again we're used to children,' she said. 'They're often frightened if they wake from the anaesthetic and find themselves in the tent and they try to fight their way out. So we make a game of it beforehand. If we have more than one here we have them putting one another into it. But obviously you don't need such treatment.'

A little to my regret she folded it back against the head of the bed. But not before I had noticed something. The tent was not new and had developed cracks here and there. These had been stuck over with adhesive plaster, and one of the strips had some writing on it 'C.G.H.T. in here 23-11-49.' He was still following me around.

Visiting hour came and my parents with it, for a last look. My father had flown up from Christchurch for the occasion, bringing with him a dark suit in case of a funeral, as I later learned. When they had gone I had a visit from the anaesthetist. He had read in my reports that I had once had an infection in the jaw and was anxious to be assured that it didn't prevent me from opening my mouth. I demonstrated, and he was satisfied. He assured me in his turn that I should have no suffocating face-mask to put me out, just a prick and I would be off. He didn't tell me what he meant to do to me after that – except that he wanted to be able to open my mouth wide. He was followed by Mr N., the Surgeon-in-Charge, a debonair young man with a bow tie and an airy walk. He came to see that I was all ready and prepared and happy. Finally, after tea, the house surgeon arrived to insert a drip into my left wrist. He chatted about Taranaki as he carved into the vein, and told me his name was Browning.

'Any relation to the poet?' I asked him.

'No, we have no relations in New Zealand,' he said; and he left me with a bottle of saline solution flowing in to keep up the blood-pressure. And then I lay, trussed up and ready, twelve hours ahead.

The rooms in one end of the ward were occupied by men, in the other end by women, and it was part of the provision for blue-babies that the room with the oxygen tent was in the female end of the ward. A woman patient was usually in the other bed to help keep an eye on the child. They didn't go as far as that for me; but as I lay there a middle-aged woman in a green dressing-gown poked her head through the window from the balcony. She asked pardon for intruding, but I looked so lonely; and she kept me occupied for some time with an account of her complicated sufferings following a motor accident. I was grateful to her.

A nurse came with a green capsule to make me sleep, and, for part of the night, I slept.

The morning was Wednesday, the 28th of June. It was pouring with rain, I believe, but I didn't notice that. I was occupied with other thoughts. I had no clear impression of anything that happened after I was wheeled down to the theatre, chiefly because my glasses were left in the locker again. A large lamp glittered above me. Figures dressed entirely in green, green-hooded, green-masked, loomed over me and then vanished. Voices asked me to lift my head, or to lower it. The saline drip was replaced by a blood transfusion, so that I could lose some of my own without damage, an event I noticed by a red and heavy smell in my nostrils, a buzzing in my ears. My limbs began to feel heavy, and when I tried to move my arm it felt as if it were attached to my side by sticking-plaster, which I had not the energy to part. This did not surprise me, although I knew there was no sticking-plaster. I had read of the use in heart operations of the South American arrow-poison, curare, to relax the muscles. Finally the voice of the anaesthetist spoke from a shadow at my side.

'Just a little prick,' he said, 'and you'll be asleep.' He injected the pentothal.

It is misleading to make a pause here, because I was aware of no interruption of consciousness at all following this injection. But I have to believe there was an interruption, of about six hours. For six hours I had no worries at all, and knew nothing of what was worrying others. I knew nothing of my parents' troubles in getting to the hospital for their long wait, on a morning the transport workers had chosen to strike in protest against Mr Holland's reduction in food subsidies. I did not see my aunt waiting for news at her flat, who had been told that if the operation were unsuccessful it would be likely to be known early, by, say, 9.30. I did not see her when the telephone rang at 9.30, and proved to be an innocent friend who knew nothing of the matter.

Nor did I know anything of the surgeons' worries when they thought at first they were not going to succeed. The subclavian artery which they intended to detach from its normal duties and graft on to the pulmonary artery beyond the constriction, was going to prove, they thought when they first looked at it, too short to serve the purpose. I did not even know anything of their pleasure when they overcame the difficulty, and when I continued alive under their hand the whole morning. I slept, and did not know I slept.

Six

I was wishing the anaesthetic would get on with the job and not keep me waiting so long, when I became aware of a pain in my chest which had not been there a minute or two before. At the same time I realised I was in the oxygen tent. I had not time to grasp what this meant before Mr N. spoke to me, asked me how I felt now they'd done it.

'Have you done it?' I asked. I couldn't believe it.

'For a time we didn't think we were going to be able to,' he said, 'but we have.' He brought my mother and father into the room.

'Well, speak to him, he can hear you,' he said, after they had stood for a moment looking at me through the plastic, watching me gasp like a fish just landed on a river bank, unable to grasp that the tent did not entirely cut me off. They spoke, and then the Sister bustled them away because I had to keep doing breathing exercises.

There was a lot to be got through yet, but they'd succeeded in doing what they meant to do, I knew that. I found as I awoke to my surroundings that I was firmly held down by the tent tucked into the blankets, my wrist was still linked to a drip by a rubber tube, and two larger tubes ran from my back over the side of the bed, where (I discovered later) they ended up in two large bottles of disinfectant, draining the lung. The nurse who was sitting by asked what I wanted for my tea. I suggested an eggflip. She brought it in a feeding cup with a spout and handed it in through a zip in the tent; and afterwards I subsided into a vague state between sleeping and waking, hardly able to care yet that what I had set out to have done was done, but knowing all the same; from which I was fully awakened at intervals during the night by two Sisters who came to watch my progress, to inject penicillin and streptomycin, and to make me cough. The cough was to help clear and expand the lung which had been deflated during the operation. I coughed as well as I could. They were shocked.

'That's no cough,' they said. 'Give a real cough.' I did my best, but I had not been in the habit of having chest coughs and I was out of practice. The two Sisters remained disgusted with me, and adjusted the drip, evidently assuming while they did it that I had gone to sleep again, for they entertained me by exchanging opinions about other members of the staff who were on duty that night.

When the Sister arrived on duty the following morning she announced the end of my invalidity in at least one respect. I was to go on a full diet immediately. Until then in hospital I had been fed on chicken, fish, offal and eggs: now I chewed my way through steaks, mutton chops, oxtail stews, whose seasoning seared my mouth and throat, still raw from the activities of the anaesthetist (he had also chipped the corner of a tooth, and, or so I thought then, permanently dislocated my uvula). I was also handicapped in my eating by being unable to use my left arm. I hadn't noticed it the previous day: the physiotherapist surprised me now when she picked it up from where it lay idly at my side and said, 'You can't do much with this, can you?' and I found I couldn't do anything with it. The muscles controlling it had been cut through to get at the ribs, and they had to be re-educated. She moved it up and down and left it alone for the rest of the day. 'But,' she said, 'we aim to get it above your head in a week.' She turned her attention to the

Right: At about six months, with my mother Margery, sister Kitty and brother Jock

Left: 'I might live to about eight, with luck.' At four, with the girl next door. Margaret is carrying a doll, I a security blanket

Below: Paddling in a pullover surrounded by kids in togs. A 1935 coarse-screen newspaper photo of Sumner School in the surf

Right: The bicycle. 'I forced their hand by saving up for it'

Below: The house in Papanui soon after it was built, before the garden was established; my window, top right

Left: Still the occasional sortie out at thirteen. Had probably been to Woolworths or McKenzies

Below left: 'Printed on a handpress.' The magazine called *Magazine*, 1943

Below: The view from my window

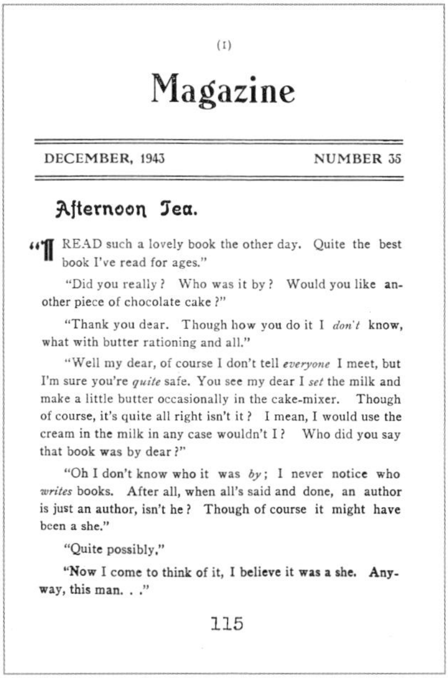

(1)

Magazine

DECEMBER, 1943 NUMBER 35

Afternoon Tea.

"I READ such a lovely book the other day. Quite the best book I've read for ages."

"Did you really? Who was it by? Would you like another piece of chocolate cake?"

"Thank you dear. Though how you do it I *don't* know, what with butter rationing and all."

"Well my dear, of course I don't tell *everyone* I meet, but I'm sure you're *quite* safe. You see my dear I *set* the milk and make a little butter occasionally in the cake-mixer. Though of course, it's quite all right isn't it? I mean, I would use the cream in the milk in any case wouldn't I? Who did you say that book was by dear?"

"Oh I don't know who it was *by*; I never notice who *writes* books. After all, when all's said and done, an author is just an author, isn't he? Though of course it might have been a she."

"Quite possibly,"

"Now I come to think of it, I believe it was a she. Anyway, this man. . ."

115

Right: The gardener from Caithness, Jim Cormack

Below: Aged about seventeen. This dim photograph (Box Brownie, no flash, fixed exposure) was the only one ever taken of me in bed

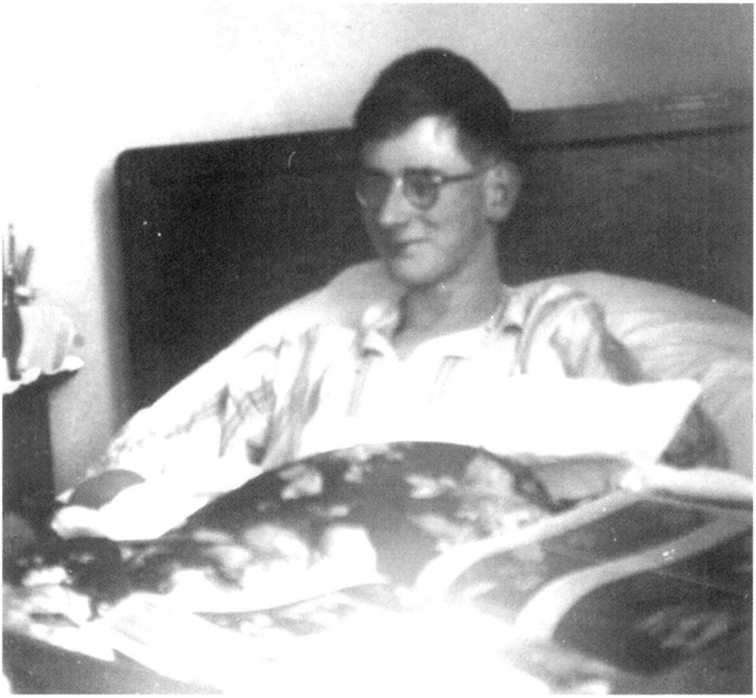

Left: Aged nineteen, with my niece Barbara

Below: 'I sat upright like a human being.' Christmas 1949, between my father and mother; Jock, Barbara, and Margaret on right

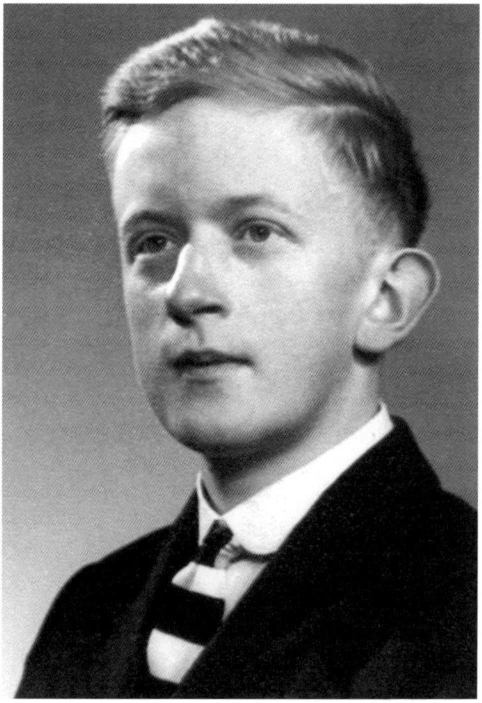

Right: 'A boy at Christ's College . . . young T.': Howard Tripp COURTESY MARGARET TRIPP

Below: Christchurch Hospital in the spring (though I was there in the summer) JOHN CHAMBERS

Above: 'A splendid example of the modern conception of a hospital.' Green Lane Hospital

Below: 'Watching the ferries float across.' From my aunt's window, Bayswater

Right: 'Smiling as if she was pleased to see us.' Mary Smaill, Sister in Charge of the Cardio-Surgical Clinic

Below: Members of the Clinic: Douglas Robb, back left; Carl Gilberd, Superintendent, front left

breathing exercises, pressing in, pushing out, in one place after another, showing how by taking thought I could direct the breath into any part of the lungs I wanted. Then she told me to cough and showed the same horror at the result as the Sisters had done in the night. I asked her *how* to cough, to describe the process, to analyse its movements. She paused for thought, made a tentative attempt to talk about the diaphragm, and then had to admit that well really she didn't know how one coughed; one just coughed.

Mr R. came to see me, accompanied by Mr N., by the Surgical Registrar and by the rest of his retinue. He showed pleasure, declared there was no more need of the oxygen tent; but cautioned me not to get too excited about the result. They had overcome the blueness, he said, but they could not promise how much of the weakness would go. The operation, he was careful to impress on me, and on my parents, was not a cure. I could never be normally active. But though he was careful to inspire no false hopes, he was not less pleased than I was about what they had done so far. A friend of my father's who was staying with him at the time described him as 'elated'.

The aftermath of a heart operation is not much different, to the patient, from any other operation, except that recovery is usually quicker, especially with the child patients. For an adult it was a little more prolonged, and I was the oldest patient they had so far operated on for Fallot's tetralogy in New Zealand. 'The first fortnight after an operation is always the worst,' people told me, a thought which consoled me during the first days when even the picture of a more active life in the future began to recede a little before the immediate fact of pain, which could only be alleviated to a certain extent because I could not be allowed to get sleepy and sluggish in breathing; of weakness and sleepless nights, when shadows in the silent ward enlarged themselves into terrors. But if my spirits began to flag they soon revived when the Superintendent popped in to tell me how well I was getting on, and the afternoon supervising sister stayed a while to tell me about this former blue-baby who was riding a bicycle and that one who was going to learn dancing; and Mr N. came in to laugh at me. He seemed often to find me funny, especially when I was not meaning to be. It was a little puzzling: but I was glad to give him pleasure.

That first week or so my brain refused to function as it ought. I had asked the physiotherapist her name the day before the operation; some days afterwards I found I was confidently calling her something quite different. I wanted to report to my parents when they came in the afternoon what the doctors had told me in the morning, but I had forgotten. I couldn't remember the date of the operation. I knew it was on a Wednesday (they were all on either Wednesday or Saturday); and had to note the date on a newspaper the following week and work backwards. Even that was not easy: when I first tried to read the paper my eyes would not focus on the words, would not form them into intelligible patterns. Not that it mattered much. The war in Korea was of minor interest to me then.

But little by little my head cleared. I began to accumulate a drawerful of fanmail from friends who had heard of the successful operation, letters, even a few telegrams; and I was soon able to read even the longest letters and absorb the delight of everyone, though they had a tendency to bring tears to my eyes which baffled and ashamed me. The one I liked best was written to my father from one of his friends who was then in Paparua prison. 'I can imagine', he wrote, 'just how excited you are, knowing that there is a good chance that your son may soon be able to get around and enjoy life to the full the same as we are able to do.'

Blue-babies were still news, and even people I scarcely knew got excited about it. In the Bay of Plenty, where a young relative of mine went to school, the news that a grown-up second cousin of hers had had a blue-baby operation caused an argument in the staff room where one of the teachers declared it wasn't possible. The indignant young cousin took a letter from my aunt to school to prove it. Even in the hospital it was still something to be a blue-baby, especially among the other patients. After several days I was moved into another room where the second bed was occupied by a Jugoslav who had been operated on for a sliding diaphragmatic hernia, whatever that might be. When he had visitors, and after he had described to them his own condition in Jugoslav or English, and sometimes both, he introduced them to me.

'I always read about a blue-baby,' he said, 'but I never knew what a blue-baby was before.' I was not clear that he knew even then, but he evidently considered a sight of me was enough.

The first fortnight *was* the worst. After that things perceptibly eased. I began to feel not only better than I had been since the operation, but better than I had been before it. There was only one setback, when suddenly, unaccountably, my temperature went up again. I knew it had, and glanced at the thermometer before the nurse returned for it. When the nurse read it she went to see the charge nurse: I could see the tops of their caps nodding towards each other through the glass panel in the door. (The panel was so high up that people who wished to see through it had to stand on tip toe, except Mr R., whose face smiled and nodded into us as his body walked past.) Next morning my temperature was still up. The surgeons gathered around, listened to my chest, asked questions, and could find nothing to account for it. There had been some fluid on the lung earlier, but this had dissipated of its own accord, and there was no sign of its returning. They were baffled.

'We'll get the physicians to see you,' they said.

Later the same morning I was surrounded by another group of doctors, chest specialists to a man. They went through the same routine, could find nothing wrong, whispered among themselves, but had no suggestions to make except that I should have an X ray. It was not until they had gone that I became aware that the generalised ache I had felt in my chest and throat since the operation had become localised and intensified. I took my shaving mirror from the drawer, peered down my throat, and found white spots on my tonsils. I was having an attack of tonsillitis. I gave the word to the Sister, the anxiety of the doctors was relieved, the X-ray orderly was sent back when he came for me, and I was put on the penicillin list again.

Meanwhile, the physiotherapist had achieved her object of getting my arm above my head a week after the operation. She began by telling me to put my hands together in an attitude of prayer; then with the right hand to assist the left to raise itself, pushing it up the first day or two, giving it moral support for a few more days; until with a tremendous effort, to which it gave a grudging and sluggish response, I could lift it above my head under its own power. It wasn't long before I forgot there had been anything wrong with it. The physiotherapist was proud of achieving this with all her patients. She had seen a film of the same operation in America, and there the patient still could not lift his arm after six weeks. 'But physiotherapy is very backward in America,' she said. She herself was English.

My left arm, besides losing its muscle power, had also lost its original circulation, because the left subclavian artery, whose job is to supply that arm with blood, had been appropriated to supply the lungs; but the blood had quickly found its way back to the arm through other channels – had established a collateral circulation, was how they put it – and I had no discomfort on that score. The only difference it made was that I had no pulse in my left wrist, which made it fun to hand that wrist to the nurse when she came along with her watch in her hand. Her face would become puzzled, then alarmed. After I had put it across them the second or third time – for in their hurry they almost never remembered – their curses were something to wonder at.

The physiotherapist then concentrated on getting me generally active, giving me a rubber strap to extend with my feet when I was lying in bed, telling me, when I was up, to sit in a chair and stand up again immediately, sit and stand, an increasing number of times; luring me to walk a little further than I thought I could, and then making me walk back to the chair. We sometimes had these sessions on the balcony on a frosty morning, and we relaxed by making up rhymes about polar bears and polar airs. She and her assistants travelled about the hospital, the three of them doing all the wards. They peered into the rooms as they passed, never disturbed a patient when he was asleep, would often leave him even if he seemed engrossed in reading.

Towards the end of my stay I was wheeled into the lift and up to the physiotherapy department on the fourth floor every morning, where I bounced rubber balls and threw darts and quoits.

The doctors at Green Lane hadn't the usual medical reticence about other cases on their hands. If Mr R. had been doing an operation he thought would interest me, he told me about it. Not many other blue-babies were around when I was there. The supply of our particular kind was beginning to run short. But there was one bright six-year-old who was running around the ward blue for a day or two and within a surprisingly short time was running around as cheerfully as ever, pink.

There was an even greater achievement in the offing. One afternoon the Sister brought a patient from the other end of the ward to see me: a slight, fair girl in a red dressing gown, with just the faintest underlining of blue to a pale complexion, who sat in the wicker chair by my bed, drew her legs up under her and squatted while she talked to me, shyly. She had been under the Cardio-Surgical Clinic for some time and they had tried to help her with physiotherapy but had not risked an operation. Now they had taken their courage in their hands and had brought her into the hospital to beat my record as the oldest patient to be given a Blalock operation in New Zealand. I had been told she was 32, but I would have said she was ten years younger. In fact, as I discovered later, she was five years older than I had been told. She was bought along to me because it was thought that to see a patient who had gone safely through the same ordeal she was facing would be good for her morale. She was not operated on for another week or so and by that time I had left the hospital. It was a famous success and on account of her great age made headlines in the newspapers.

These were exciting times in Green Lane. While I was there a boy in his twenties had his spleen removed to relieve an anaemic condition. It was the first operation of its kind in New Zealand. A man in his sixties was operated on for an aneurism of the aorta, a fatal disease previously, and this was one of the first of its kind in New Zealand. He was soon home, leaving behind him a reputation for having the largest appetite for bread-and-butter the nurses had ever encountered. Lung operations for Tb were also being done but I didn't see these patients. They were kept in their own block, a three-storey building evidently about half-way in age between the medical wards I had left and the main block I was now in, a grey shadowy pile in forbidding unpainted concrete. Our only lung operation was for cancer: the patient had so little lung left after it that he had to keep rubber tubes from an oxygen cylinder constantly in his mouth, hardly able to remove them even to eat. The oxygen came hissing from the cylinder, but still it wasn't enough; he turned the gauge on fuller, and anxiously watched the needle on the dial as it dropped towards zero, panicking when he thought the replacement cylinder wasn't going to arrive before the other was empty. He died the day I left hospital.

For the last fortnight I shared a room with a man in his fifties who was dying of cancer of the gullet. He told me about it, calmly and directly, soon after I had been moved in with him. He had been troubled with difficulty in swallowing for several years, had seen doctor after doctor, had been X-rayed time after time; and nothing was revealed which would account for the symptoms. Nerves, he was told; and when finally it became too clear that it wasn't just nerves and he was opened up it was too late. He showed no bitterness: he hoped his experience would make early diagnosis easier in other cases.

When I first saw him he was still getting up to bath and shave, to ring his wife, and to sit in the sun. He talked to me until my eyelids drooped and his voice became meaningless, he listened to the radio, he read, he had a bottle of sherry in his wardrobe which he shared with one or two favourite nurses. He could not eat, but he could still drink tea, and thin soup, and orange juice, and a pain-relieving concoction known as Mr N.'s cocktail, of which he had a high opinion. He always timed his afternoon dose to take effect during the visiting hour, so that he should appear at his brightest.

He grew rapidly worse. He declined as I advanced: and he kept a warm and kindly eye on my advance and gave me advice about the world. The day I had my first bath was the day he, reluctantly, first had a sponge in bed. As I was able to sit out of bed more, he was able to sit out of bed less. He grew less talkative, I grew more. As I had more pleasure from listening to his radio, he was able to stand it on less and less. During the first few days I was in the room he would do little bits of fetching and carrying for me about the room; during the last few days I was fetching things for him.

The time came when he was no longer able to keep down his cups of tea or his orange juice, or, worst blow of all, Mr N.'s cocktail. He was depressed that day. He had known it was coming, but it came earlier than he had expected, or hoped. But he refused the chance of being kept alive a little longer by artificial feeding. He preferred to die of starvation rather than wait for the spreading cancer to reach more vital parts. He had a visitor that evening, a fellow member of the Orphans Club, who stood on one foot and then on the other, saying periodically, 'Well, Joe . . .' and, 'Yes, Joe . . .' while Joe said very little and grew more and more weary.

'Well, Joe,' his visitor said, finally, 'the boys will be glad to hear how you are.'

'Then you'd better tell them to start saving their sixpences.'

'Why, Joe?'

'For the wreath.'

The fellow Orphan shifted from one foot to the other a few more times.

'Well, Joe,' he said, 'it's no use beating about the bush, is it? As man to man we *know*, don't we, Joe?'

'Yes,' said Joe, 'and now, if you don't mind, I'm very tired . . .'

One of the student nurses was a Catholic; she came into the room one day and said she had been telling the Sisters at her old convent school about his courage, and they had sent him some pamphlets to read. He accepted them graciously and put them in his locker. He didn't read them; but he had no fears for the future. He told me he had never knowingly harmed anyone; he had always tried to do the best by other people; and he was sure God would do the same by him. That was his religion, he said.

He lay asleep one morning, emaciated, yellow, exhausted. The young wardsmaid sweeping the room leaned on her broom and gazed at him with large, gloomy eyes.

'He hasn't long for this world,' she said.

'I know,' I said. 'So does he.'

'Does he know?' she said. 'It's a funny thing, they always tell them in this place.'

She loathed this place. Green Lane was so *morbid*, she said; and she was so impressed by the fact that she carried from room to room stories of this one who was dying in that room and the other whose operation was unsuccessful on the floor above. The day after my operation when I was still scarcely awake from it she had gazed at me with those same large eyes and wondered how anyone could consent to have a heart operation, it was so *dangerous*.

Now I was indignant. Even my room mate did not strike me as being morbid, and Green Lane certainly did not. How could it, when I had gained a new life there? It was a cheerful place: the doctors were cheerful, the nurses were cheerful, the other wardsmaids were cheerful, the other patients were – well, mostly cheerful. Only one wardsmaid was not, and she said *Green Lane* was morbid. It did not occur to me to wonder whether she might be right and the rest of us wrong.

Yet in spite of myself I was not enjoying watching the other man sink lower as I rose higher, like an illustration of the see-saw of life. I was glad, and ashamed that I was glad, that the time for my discharge was near. Green Lane was a good place, a splendid hospital, but it was time I was out of it. As I vacated my bed the man in the other was wheeled into a single room to die. He lasted another fortnight.

Seven

I was to convalesce in Bayswater for a month before I flew back to Christchurch. The doctors advised me to fly this time with every confidence. In the meantime, for the journey across the harbour to Bayswater I travelled for the last time by ambulance.

It was when I was back in a private home, in a private routine, that I began to realise fully what they had done for me, even at this early stage. Little things, like dressing, even brushing my hair, which had once been almost intolerably fatiguing, now came easily. I could talk to visitors for much longer without tiring. A morning or two after I had moved from Green Lane I stood on the back doorstep of the flat looking over the harbour to the city and up the harbour past Watchman Island to the Waitakeres on the horizon, watching the ferries cleaving through the lines of sunlight lying across the water, noticing how the skyline of Auckland was dominated by the spires of churches and of giant Norfolk Island pines. I had stood there for some minutes before I woke up to the fact that I was standing there, *standing,* where a month ago I could not possibly have stood long enough to take anything in.

I began to learn to live in the world: and I quickly found the world did not lie open to me. It had to be conquered. This meant

I was constantly confronted by things I was scared to do, and after a decent interval for meditating and resolving I had to do them. One of the first of these was having a bath, in a bath. I began it in hospital, naturally enough; for in a hospital cleanliness ranks a long way above godliness, and the first bath is the baptism to which the catechumen is hurried as quickly as it is safe to go, with a fervour which I am sure must have descended in hospital tradition from the time when it was rare for anyone to have a bath except in a hospital. Most of the world now agrees with hospitals, about the luxury as well as the virtue of bathing in a bath. 'How you must love having a bath,' my friends said, knowing it was years since my breath had allowed me to do it.

I did enjoy having a bath – after a time. At first I sat rigid in the water and clung to the rim with one hand while I soaped desperately with the other. Then I began to relax, and to discover things. When I had washed from a basin on my bed I had washed, and that was all there was to it. But in a bath, I discovered, washing was only a pretext: the real reason for having a bath was to do all the things that can only be done in a bath. I discovered how to make a little air-filled balloon of the face-cloth, to plunge it under the water and let the air escape through the weave, squeezing it out in a stream of tiny bubbles or in one great splash all at once. I have not yet met anyone else who can do this.

And I sailed the two halves of a celluloid soap-dish, rocked them with waves, swamped them, capsized them, emptied them out and started again; swamping one gently this time, to discover just how much water it would hold without sinking. I stippled the side of the bath with water from the nail-brush. I longed for a yellow, rubber, floating duck. But the duck, when I got it, did not come up to my expectation. It was an unsatisfactory, characterless creature. It capsized too easily, it refused to be controlled, it left yellow stains on the window-sill – I was bored by it. For a long time it sat in the bathroom gathering dust against the ridges of its pretended feathers, ignored even by my small nieces and nephew, and it finally perished, unnoticed, unlamented.

As I matured in experience I left off wanting a pop-pop boat and even began to relegate the face-cloth, the soap-dish and the nail-brush to the purposes their manufacturers intended them for. I now began to perceive the true use of the bath was for thinking; a use I was able to appreciate the more as I found less time for thinking anywhere else. Bathing is one of the degenerate luxuries which are supposed to have caused the downfall of the Roman civilisation; but as long as it remains with us predominantly a solitary occupation it may yet prove the salvation of ours by forcing it to face up to itself and think. This is a thought I thought up in the bath.

Having a bath required will-power, but it could not be said to be intellectually demanding. The trouble there was *running* the bath. It wouldn't have been so bad if there had only been one tap with a mixture of standard warmth, but there were two of the things.

'Run a little hot in first,' I was told, 'or the bath will be chilly to sit upon. But not too much at once,' I was further told, 'or you'll scald yourself if you fall in.' So I did as I was bid and ran a little hot and dipped my finger in and pulled it out again quick and turned on some cold and dipped and turned on some hot and bobbed up and down like a chicken pecking corn. This constant necessity for making judgments nearly brought on nervous exhaustion every morning; but fortunately after a time I noticed some minute flaws in the enamel on the surface of the bath, little pits and bumps at strategic intervals. Hot water run to the first of these, h. and c. both to the second and cold alone to the third made a good average bath. The relief was enormous and entirely compensated for the odd uncomfortable day when the cold was a bit colder than usual or the hot a bit hotter. This system lasted some time; but if anyone were to ask me now how I run my bath I don't think I could tell them. As far as I'm concerned it just happens.

But I never realised the capacity of the human mind for truly intricate remembering and reasoning until I first began to make a pot of tea. The number of things there were to remember! To turn on the kettle, to make sure there was some water in the kettle, to find a tray cloth, to find it was the wrong size and find another one, to find the cups and the saucers to go with cups, and the saucer that most nearly went with the odd cup. To hear the kettle boiling and to turn it off until I was ready for it. To sniff the milk, to pour some fresh milk into a clean jug, and replace the cap on the milk-bottle, to take the sugar from the cupboard and then to put it back again because nobody took sugar. And that was before I even began to brew the stuff. The person who could master the moves of a two or three course dinner must have had the brain of a Rutherford, I thought then, and I still think. But I *can* boil an egg and make mint sauce.

When I had made a cup of tea, drinking it was pleasant enough. Achievement sharpened the flavour. That was just drinking a cup of tea. But before I had even begun to make tea, I made the acquaintance of another matter altogether – the *afternoon tea.* And not only at home, but out. For I paid my first call, on two very good friends, who lived on the other side of the narrow Bayswater peninsula – which meant they lived two streets away.

I had been in Auckland five years before when I first met them. My mother was ill and I had gone to Auckland to be looked after by my aunt for several months. A friend had come to visit my aunt and my aunt brought her to my room to visit me. She was – well I never did ask her age, it was uncertain. She was dressed for walking with brogues and a stout stick and she had put scent somewhere about her. I was rolling cigarettes for my aunt with a patent machine someone had given her and as each one popped from the hole she picked it up, held each end to her nose and sighed that it smelt beautiful. She would dearly love to smoke, she said, but she knew if once she started she would never stop, so she didn't dare start. Her husband was a radio announcer, and as we talked we listened and she punctuated his announcements with 'yes, dear,' and 'that's quite right, dear.' We soon found that we liked one another and liked many of the same things.

She and her husband had visited my bedside both in Auckland and in Christchurch, and when they were in one place and I in the other we had written. I knew, as I thought, just about everything there was to know about them; but all I knew in fact was a shadow, an emanation from their true life which they lived in their house on the other side of the Bayswater peninsula. I could not guarantee that in fact they lived in a house at all, or that when their retreating footsteps echoed up the path of an evening they were not disappearing from life, as well as from my life.

Now I was driven to their house and, stopped before it, found it not at all as I had imagined it, partly because I had not really imagined it at all; but also because if I had I should not have imagined the door just *there* or the windows just so. I was out of the car, stepping over the pungent onion-weed on the roadside, through the gate, down the sloping path, to the front door, to the bell which would not ring, to her wide-flung arms – the same arms which had come out a little prematurely a few minutes before and had only just saved themselves from embracing a surprised telegraph boy. And then I was sitting in the living-room, looking down from the window to a quiet backwater of the harbour, ready to learn how my friends lived at home.

I had not calculated on the afternoon tea; and from the moment it was wheeled in I could absorb nothing but the torture of it. Strangely enough none of the others seemed to find it torture. They quietly, easily, mastered their flesh, while I balanced mine with difficulty upright in an armchair, holding on that uneasy balance a cup of tea in one hand (best bone china, and won't you have another cup) and a plate of food on the left kneecap, leaving the other hand free to rove from one to the other or gesticulate as required. Being fed with airy fancies that collapsed at a touch and oozed everywhere. Remembering to eat now and then and drink now and then and carry on the conversation between.

'Is that,' sip munch, 'that one of,' munch sip, 'of his pictures?' sip munch sip, and there goes some whipped cream on the carpet or a tomato slice on the moquette and I was trying to solve the pretty problem of whether it showed better breeding to disown and repudiate the shame, or to dab at it surreptitiously with a handkerchief. My clothes were wet with the effort of the occasion, and I couldn't say I had yet absorbed much of the way of life of my friends at home. Yet it was something to assure myself that they did live in a house, on that afternoon at least, and not in a cave or up a tree. And it was something to have accomplished the first afternoon tea.

For even with afternoon teas the technique was gradually learned, and the agony passed; and it was only a couple of months afterwards that I afternoon-tead on equal terms with a Minister of the Crown, than whom there is no one in better training when it comes to afternoon teas. And not long after that I discovered it was possible with careful management to have one's own afternoon tea at home and casually call on a neighbour in time for another. Say not the struggle naught availeth. All the same the household extravagance I most approve of is a nest of tables.

There was only one topic of conversation then and for a long time afterwards, my operation. I talked about it, or if I did not know the people well enough myself I modestly withdrew to a corner with a book and let my parents talk about it. We learned to gauge the sensitivity of our audiences, after one man to whom my parents had described the operation of a cardiac catheter had gone outside to be sick on the flowerbed. On the other hand there were those who could take any amount of detail, and who did so wish they could have been there to see it.

There were those who had different questions. 'Wasn't it,' they would ask delicately, 'very pricey?' They were relieved, or sometimes perhaps a little disappointed, to know that it hadn't cost us a penny, apart from our share of Social Security tax.

I am not sure that at first our descriptions of the operation were very accurate. The doctors had told us what they were doing in fairly general terms in consideration for our medical ignorance. My mother did once appeal to one of them to draw a *simple diagram*. 'The trouble is,' he said, 'that it's really rather complicated.' I had heard the doctors talking about it but did not know enough of their vocabulary to interpret what they said. Gradually, however, as I was able to read some literature on the subject (found by my brother in the National Library Service collection), to study some of the necessary anatomy, and to look up some of the words I had heard most frequently the picture began to grow, I hoped, a little more accurate. The meaning of the word 'anastomosis' eluded me for some time; I forgot to make allowance for the local accent and was looking up 'enestomosis.'

After a time, I will confess, being a curiosity palled. I grew resentful that people seemed to want to meet me as an exhibit. I said so to a friend. 'At least it's better than being in a jar in the pathology lab.,' he said; and I have no doubt he was right.

The month at Bayswater was up, and I was at Whenuapai waiting to board the plane for Christchurch. A Colonel and a Brigadier who were organising K Force dumped their portfolios beside me while they went and drank a cup of tea, and I missed a chance to do some private spying, but my mind was still on other things. I could not yet walk far and it was therefore necessary to ask for a chair to wheel me over the tarmac to the plane, and to do this it was necessary to do some explaining. There were anxious conferences. The pilot was informed and came along. Did the doctor know, he asked my mother, that I was flying? When he was told the doctor had recommended it, he allowed, but with obvious misgivings, that I might fly on his plane. The airport hostess wheeled up the chair, a beautiful contraption all springs and foam rubber and tubular steel, and I was put aboard, with the old ladies and the babes in arms. The co-pilot when he came aboard told me they would fly as low as possible, but could not, unfortunately, fly *very* low; but if I felt in any way distressed, or too hot or too cold, I must ring the bell and they would do what they could. Later the pilot came along and repeated the instructions. The attention was kind and flattering, but it came at a time when it was no longer necessary, and I had a good easy flight home.

My sister had come to town from the country to meet us. Her three-year-old Richard had a long look at me.

'Dennis woke up,' he said.

Eight

In hospital I had thought of that first summer at home: a summer to be spent, when I was not doing the more active things I intended to do, sitting on the lawn under the trees, lazing my way into strength. Very soon after I returned I commissioned my father to bring a chair home from town; a low chair with padded canvas cushions resting on a webbing of rope, the whole supported by two red wooden wheels in front and two legs at the back, so that it could be wheeled like a wheelbarrow to whichever part of the garden it was wanted. This was the chair in which I meant to spend the summer, sitting under the trees on the lawn.

Things didn't work out like that. For one thing there was very little summer that summer, and sitting on the lawn under the trees was not so attractive when a Christchurch easterly was whistling through the branches. But the main trouble was the sky. The sky was too big. For years I had lived under a ceiling: even on my rare outings I had travelled in an enclosed car. Now when I sat under the sky, in a few minutes my head grew light, I felt dizzy and as if I was going to fall, I wanted to press myself to the earth and crawl to shelter. I did not even have to look at the sky for this to happen, nor even to be consciously aware that I was under it. It happened, and I had to retreat inside.

The only comfort was that I was evidently not the first person to be affected so. I read Joyce Cary's *The Horse's Mouth* and came upon this on the first page: 'They say a chap just out of prison runs into the nearest cover; into some dark little room, like a rabbit put up by a stoat. The sky feels too big for him. But I liked it. I swam in it.' Maybe Jimson did like it; but he had not been in prison long enough. You don't find the sky too big when you've only been away from it for a month.

I tried sitting out for five minutes, then for ten, and so to learn gradually to tolerate the sky; but this didn't work. To sit under the sky with such calculation made me too aware of what I was doing and brought on the giddiness sooner and more completely. The only thing I could do was to humour the phobia, to keep under cover meantime, and to wait and see what happened.

For a long time nothing happened. I began to fear I should have to spend the rest of my life under a ceiling. I was quite safe on a veranda, and that was where I spent the days I had hoped to spend on the lawn. I could even feel protected by an overhanging cave; but emerge from it and I was done. Even a high ceiling troubled me. I went to see a play at the Theatre Royal in Christchurch. My seat was booked in the front stalls. I looked up – and had to retreat ignominiously to the back stalls under the shelter of the circle, distressing the usher that I was not getting the full value of the seat I had paid for. Fortunately for me, though not for Ngaio Marsh's Commonwealth Theatre party, it was not a full theatre.

It was only when I tried to *sit* under it that the sky worried me. It did not keep me from walking, so long as I did not tempt it too blatantly, by walking for instance across a paddock. To walk along by a fence was better, better still a hedge, something for the mind to hang on to, for the tips of the fingers to run along, to assure myself it was there. If there was no fence, still a path was better than no path, a line to guide the feet, a prescribed way, to keep me from plunging into the void.

It was a long time, eighteen months, before the sky began to release its oppression. Then one morning I walked along the road to visit the newly inducted Presbyterian minister in his newly built Manse. I found him digging the garden. A working bee from the church had dug over the property with a rotary hoe and had built the paths; but the part of the backyard on which the shingle and cement had been dumped had missed the hoe and the minister was digging it. He was not used to digging. He puffed, he groaned; and passing a hand over a damp forehead as I appeared he welcomed someone to talk to and erected a deckchair for me nearby. Not wanting to go into long explanations, I sat in it, and watched him dig and sat in it. The sky was overhead and I sat under it and it held its peace. We talked about the symbolism of the communion and about George MacLeod and the Iona Community. He puffed even more than before from the effort of talking while he dug; his wife passed in and out of the wash-house carrying baskets of clothes to the line – it was Monday morning; a ginger cat, almost white, with one paw left behind in a rabbit trap, lay in the sun nearby; and I sat happily and unconcernedly under the sky; until at last the minister tired of digging and took me inside to drink iced lime juice.

Not wanting to go into long explanations I did not tell him what had been happening that morning before his eyes without his knowing it; but, whether it was the influence of the man or of his calling, of the place or of the conversation, or whether I was ready for it in any case, I could sit under the sky thereafter. With circumspection at first. That morning I had been sitting within an angle of the house. There were walls on two sides and the garage almost enclosed another. The sky was overhead, but it was narrowly bounded: I had to proceed cautiously to enlarge those bounds. When I could sit with impunity in a quarter-acre section, my head would still object to a two-acre paddock. But I have since sat on an open riverbank, tossing round stones at a log emerging from the water, quite unable to fathom why I could never hit it, admiring the white clouds sailing over the hills. Even more recently I have several times sat without disaster on a beach, a thing I had convinced myself I should never be able to do. But I will admit that my idea of a nightmare would be to find myself in the middle of the Sahara or on top of a mountain, alone, with nothing between me and the sky. Yet strangely enough no dream has yet taken advantage of this obviously vulnerable point to give me such a nightmare. Touch wood.

Walking did not come easily either. Muscles which had lain unused so long could not immediately begin to work; but in time they hardened. What did not so soon harden, become blasé, was the excitement, the delight, the fearsome thrill of walking; and this was the greatest obstacle to increasing the distance I could walk. For some time after I could happily trot about the house and garden for what aggregated quite a distance, the idea of *going for a walk* was so exciting, so nerve-wracking, that my heart would pound, this would make me breathless, which would reduce the distance I could walk and make me more tired after it than I should have been, which would make it harder to start next time. I would worry; and knowing that worrying only made matters worse, I would worry about worrying... Mind for the moment conquered matter with a vengeance.

I had a friend, a spastic, whom I told one day that I could walk much further if I had no prior intention of walking any distance at all and just let my feet wander on, than if I set out deliberately to make new records. He knew all about it, it happened to himself: but it was strange, he thought, that I should be so affected when my disability, unlike his, was purely physical. It would have seemed strange to me, too, if I had not long ago come to the conclusion that there is no such thing as a *purely* physical disability. Even when the origin, the seat, of the trouble consists in such an undeniably physical fact as the congenital narrowing of an artery, modified by the techniques of surgery, there is in almost every particular manifestation of the disablement to the person it belongs to such a mixture of the physical, the mental and the emotional, that they can hardly be untangled. They are so intertwined that it comes to be doubtful whether they can properly be regarded as separate entities at all.

The trouble with walking was overcome in the same way as the fear of the sky: by ceasing, for a time, to struggle. It worked more quickly, too. For a couple of months I did not try to walk any distance, until the conflict was almost forgotten. Then came the morning when I put some pennies in my pocket, went quietly through the door and the gate, walked to the telephone box on the corner, and rang home.

After that walking was my recreation. It extended slowly, one further house along the street every now and then; but I was now walking not merely for the exercise but for the delight; and when I read in Mrs Wilson's *My First Eighty Years* the opinion that only the very rich could afford to walk for the sake of walking, I wondered how anyone so wise could say a thing so foolish.

I liked to pluck leaves and grasses as I passed, watching how they grew, wishing I knew their names – though I was too indolent to make an effort to find out. I saw close how the plane tree over the road dropped its bark in strips, leaving the remaining grey marbled with the yellow underbark. I saw earwigs, and found that now I was grown up, a rationalist, no longer believing that earwigs *get into your ears and kill you*, seeing earwigs had lost its earlier thrill. I saw a quince growing out of a japonica tree, and a hawthorn from a rowan; acts, I was told, not of God but of nurserymen. I heard a bird on a birch branch give a strange cry and looking saw a quail parading its topknot and its speckles and its odd black face among the bare twigs. I didn't know quails climbed trees. It skimmed down to the street after a while and ran along the footpath and around the corner into the next street. I followed, but by the time I turned the corner it was out of sight, I did not know where; nor could I imagine where it had come from.

'They're beautiful on toast,' said my mother, who had watched it from the veranda, 'but I prefer not to see them alive first.'

I picked dandelion clocks and told incredible times by them. I saw dragon-flies standing motionless on a leaf, their long bodies stretching so far back into space I wondered how they could defy gravity so. I met a hedgehog one afternoon walking infinitesimally in the middle of the street, touched it gently with my foot to make it curl into a ball and then rolled it gently to the grass verge out of the way of cars; and then saw a small girl approach it, lift it lovingly to her breast and carry it home. I began to feel acquainted with natural history.

And with people, as a part of natural history. I was shy at first of meeting people as I walked along. To be walking seemed so ostentatious, almost exhibitionist, like going around wearing a red top-hat or no trousers. I could not believe it would not seem so to others. To those people who knew me it did seem as novel and exciting to see me walk as it did to me to be walking; but I wasn't concerned about the people I knew. However, I soon found to my surprise that strangers did not stare to see me walking, and I lost my first instinct to dodge behind a hedge when I saw one coming.

I was soon on nodding and good-daying terms with many of the people around. I met people face to face whom I had known in the past as figures walking along the street or around their gardens; figures I had known intimately by their shapes, their sizes, their modes of dressing, their stances, their hairstyles, rather than by their faces, which at that distance were more imagined than seen. And now, confronted by their detail, it was often startlingly unlike the imagining – a mouth larger, a nose shorter, an eye brighter, giving an entirely different look to a person. Yet after the first astonished moments they clicked into focus and at once became part of my idea of the person. I would lean on their fences as I passed and admire their gardens and hear them all say, 'Oh there's nothing much in my garden just now; it's the wrong season. I don't do much to it in any case,' and they would get down on their knees and continue their frantic battle with nature. I would hear of their problems. The woman who was distressed to have discovered her cat lurking under the bird-bath. 'I didn't think he'd be *sneaky*,' she said, looking reproachfully, lovingly, at the sleek black monster. I tried to make friends with the cat, who wasn't having any. And the man who was cursing the twitch and cursing the neighbour who let it grow under the fence.

I remembered those speculations I had indulged in when I was confined to one place and my view was confined to a straight line from my eyes, those wonderings whether where the eye could not see there could be anything at all. I could now walk around the corners and have a look, and discover what I had scarcely believed. Neighbours' houses did have backs to them. They didn't end in a jagged edge of lath-and-plaster like a cinema mock-up. Nor did the earth drop suddenly into space behind the wash-house chimney. Cucumbers and carrots grew there. And the houses had not only fronts and backs, they had insides as well. I might have guessed it from the lights that shone forth in the night and the melodies that issued from the bathroom windows. But now I knew: they had insides furnished with refrigerators and three-piece suites and china rabbits with long ears; and unless, as might possibly be the case, this existence was entirely in the eye of the beholder and came into being when the eye was turned towards it, it seemed likely the houses always did have insides and inhabitants.

I learned to walk to the store, and to see there shelves and shelves filled with tins and cartons and packets I had scarcely dreamed I might put into my stomach. I wandered along the street in the township window-shopping, examining incredulously the jackets of the latest successes standing up in the window of the book-club; depressed by the dejection of the cakes in the cake-shop, cheered by the peacefulness of the fish in the fish-shop; horrified at the price tickets in the butcher's shop.

When I wrote a letter I went myself to the corner to post it in the box, and when I had done so I wanted to take it out again and write on it a boast in red ink. 'Look at this letter,' I wanted to write on it, 'appreciate it, treasure it, *I posted it*.' I stood on the corner and watched the cars go by, the sudden faces whirled past in square and high or round and squat frames, children in reverse peering from the back windows. I approached parked cars and after years of studying the advertisements and identifying cars from a distance by their outlines I could now really look at them and stand on tiptoe and peer and peer and gloat. I expected at any moment to be arrested on suspicion of planning to convert, and I should not have thought the suspicion grossly unfounded.

I would savour a free show in the street: a council truck breaking down and having to be towed away, or a timber truck dropping on to the roadway with a loud whang a large slab of two-by-four, which was almost immediately picked up by a following cyclist and deftly tied to the bar of his bicycle with a piece of string fished from his pocket, where he must have put it in intelligent anticipation of just such a windfall. I would watch houses being built and discover to my astonishment that waterpipes and electric wires were fixed in place before the inside walls were plastered. I had thought they were poked down through the walls afterwards as I had seen done when a new powerpoint was installed in an occupied house.

I had difficulty in remembering what I had been taught in my childhood, that it *is rude to stare*.

It was often the little things of no importance at all that seemed the most important; more important than the large and obvious entertainments anyone in bed must dream of because they came unbidden, unheralded, when I was looking the other way. Sudden unexpected delights, like holes in my socks. It seemed incredible when I found the first. A *hole* in my sock! I said to myself, not believing it, a hole in my *sock*! a hole in *my* sock! In so many years, although I had worn an acre of holes in the seats of my pyjamas, I had not worn a sock enough, with friction enough, to wear it through. And I found my shoes needed cleaning. A little dusting now and then had once sufficed. These things seemed the final proof that I was walking.

Nine

For longer explorations I had still to rely on cars. My former baby-sitter, Miss J., used now to come occasionally and take me out in her little pre-war Morris. At times she would take me to visit in her flat, and jogging along the streets between the car dipped an inquisitive nose into every rut in the road and gave one a sensation of reckless speed when the speedometer touched twenty. We would sit by the fire and drink tea and eat cake while she read me the Christmas quiz from the *Spectator* or I would recite to her the whole of the *Vicar of Bray,* which she found a little surprising, and we would deplore Dr Malan and the Americans.

On other occasions, on fine days, she and the car and I explored further afield, and in whatever the driver found interest as she drove along the car would be interested too. We drove by a tyre-factory; it looked interesting, and before we knew it the car had poked its nose into the gate, where it was met by a polite attendant who suggested that if we wished to see the factory we should join the conducted tour which started around the factory every afternoon at two. As it was then only eleven the car withdrew and proceeded further up the road until it came to a quarry where an enormous dragline was carrying shingle from a water-logged pit high into the air to the crushing tower. The car turned towards the entrance but was brought up sharply against a notice promising that Trespassers would be Prosecuted; and, backing into the roadway again, continued on its way until it arrived at the municipal airport. Here it was luckier: it could drive right to the terminal. We left it outside and went in, but found nothing to see but an occasional Tiger Moth bobbing into the air. It was one of the off periods, between the times when passenger planes arrive and depart in batches. This was a pity. I like watching other people leave by air. One keeps so calm. The magazines lay on the tables unread, the chairs were unsat on, the cakes in the cafeteria uneaten. Miss J. read the posters hanging on the walls offering trips to Fiji and Singapore and noted grammatical errors in several of them. She then proposed we should go for a drive along the runways since nothing else seemed to be using them just then. With some difficulty I argued her out of that idea, and as the next best thing we circumnavigated the aerodrome on the nearest public roads; an enjoyable but as it turned out rather rocky journey, because the 'drome had recently been extended so that it took in some parts of the roads, and they had been only roughly reformed outside the new boundary.

On another of our outings she took me to a political meeting: a rally called in Latimer Square to protest against the Police Offences Amendment Bill, at the end of 1951. None of her respectable friends would go with her, she said, so she asked me. We arrived in Latimer Square five minutes before the meeting was due to begin and found it inhabited by nothing but grass and trees and sunshine, and wondered if we had mistaken the location; but a few protesters soon ambled up, some of them carrying a pair of steps and a loudspeaker, around which clustered enough people to make it apparent they *were* clustering. Most of the audience lay on the grass, and the trees lay their shadows beside them: a peaceful scene for a threatened police state. Parents wheeled prams to and fro on the pavement while they listened for a time and then moved on. Policemen stood about and grinned when the speakers denounced the excessive powers they were given in the bill; they patted a passing baby on the head and laughed when an organiser shook a collection box under their noses. The enthusiastic Miss J. whispered to me she was glad she had left her purse at home.

The speakers mounted the steps one by one and spoke to the microphone: they had been given ten minutes each and most of them managed to restrict themselves to twenty. A lawyer read quotations from Milton and Mill; a lecturer in economics who came from Central Europe and therefore knew what he was talking about was persuasive and rational; a furious housewife from the Housewives' Union told us off straight: 'There ought to be far more of you here. You're so apathetic you'll let your liberties be filched from you without a protest'; a Marxist trades union secretary with flaring grey hair and flaming tie made a fiery speech; the most persistent writer of letters-to-the-paper in the city saw the greatest menace of the bill to lie in the possibility that editors might be discouraged from printing his letters; an Anglican clergyman disclaimed identity with any of the other speakers on any subject but the undesirability of the bill; a Presbyterian clergyman got more applause than anyone else by mounting the steps in his clerical collar and claiming to speak for the right of any man to go down the street saying to hell with the government; and also by limiting his speech to four minutes. None of the speakers was at all discouraged by the fact that the bill had already been amended to exclude most of the provisions they were objecting to.

This was my first introduction to public affairs. And carrying out thus my duties as a citizen I had my first feeling of being of some use to the community.

Driven about by my father, when he had time, I discovered more of the city, found new places, recovered for my senses more of the landscape which in the years since I had last been able to move about had been fading in memory. My eyes, undimmed by seeing them too often, were ravished by the glowing colour and shape of riverbanks grown with willows, of seats under the willows on which people leaned together, slept, looked about, read. We drove up the Cashmere Hills, and I saw the town drop below, flatten, become two-dimensional, the horizon enlarge; and at the top of Hackthorne Road was struck, as visitors from overseas proudly taken to it must have been struck, by that extraordinary phenomenon, the Sign of the Takahe. Mr Ell's little bit of old England on our tussock-covered nor'-west-swept hillside, built with loving craftsmanship by unemployed labour to represent his idea of a medieval castle, though serving the more mundane purpose of a tea-rooms, struck me as a delightful piece of beautifully executed whimsy, rather like an Emett train; but I had an uneasy suspicion that it may not have been intended to be whimsical at all, in spite of several touches of genius. The grand staircase for example. A central flight rose from the entrance hall to the lounge. On either side further flights descended to a lower floor: one of them labelled *Ladies*, the other *Gentlemen*. A medieval castle with all mod cons. There are more remarkable discoveries to be made in a modern matter-of-fact New Zealand city than will ever be known by citizens who can never make the discoveries because they knew about them all along.

I began to visit art exhibitions, walking around baffled by too many things to look at, by the inability to switch my mind efficiently from one picture to the next as my eyes moved between. In bookshops I was just as bewildered, finding myself surrounded by such an uncanny number of books that first my head went round and round and then the books went round and round. I couldn't at first see them individually at all; until my eye would seize on titles I already knew something about; and there were so many of these and they were so desirable that I could hardly help myself bundling them all up and taking them to the counter. But at least the number was itself a protection to my pocket. It was so difficult to make a choice that when I had no money anyway it was comparatively easy to choose very little. I continued to find it safer to order most of my books by mail, however; and going into bookshops remained an occasional, exhilarating, perilous adventure, to which I went well armed with a carefully compiled list of books I didn't intend to be beguiled from, and just a little extra in my pocket to allow myself the dissipation of being beguiled by a little something. There seemed to be people who could safely enter a bookshop without intending to buy anything and emerge after a time without having fallen, but I doubted if I could ever carry that off myself. I liked Christmas shopping, which gave me the excuse for an orgy; though I could find no really satisfactory compromise between buying what I thought my relatives ought to like to read and those I thought they would like to read.

Christmas – that was another stage in feeling my way into the world, for how else except in this uninhibited season could I know people were capable of behaving like that? I got my Christmas shopping done early before the rush started; for I had been warned by knowing what Christmas shopping did to my relatives in former years – when, certainly, they had to do my shopping as well as their own. They had departed soon after breakfast looking as fresh and crisp as flowers under the dew; and they had returned hours later looking as if they had been under a hot shower, limp and red and wet, with parcels hanging from every limb, and gasping for a cup of tea. In a few hours there had been such a disintegration of personality as to be terrifying to see.

So I was canny; but I wasn't going to let Christmas pass me by entirely. Although I had been warned I knew I must at least *see* the Christmas rush, and I used my need for a haircut as an excuse. It will be an experience, I told myself. So I went among the heat of the sun and the heat of the crowds, who rushed around like multicoloured ants, the mothers among them dashing along the footpaths dragging children by the hand as the Red Queen did Alice, and not really getting ahead much faster. I opened the door of the car to go among them and reeled sideways as a bicycle crashed into it – an incident passed off politely on both sides. I crossed Colombo Street, fearfully; for it was only a little while ago that I dared not cross any street at all, even if there was nobody and no vehicle in sight: and this was Colombo Street in Christmas week, even if I was protected by the lights. As I neared the haven of the other side a tram champing for the lights to let it loose closed its doors with a tremendous sigh of compressed air, and I nearly died of the shock. Then I nearly trod on a dog which lay on the pavement in a relaxed heap basking in the sun. It opened one eye and closed it again and took no further notice of me, the only tranquil creature in town. I was caught up in a rush of glowing females for a bargain line of gingham. A cup of tea gave me enough stamina to stagger back to the car, in which I was carried home in a complete disintegration of personality, wondering why I had not been warned.

School broke up. I heard voices floating from our local school about a block away, angelic voices carried on the air, singing *Silent Night.* And a few minutes later as I walked down the street to post just one more card to someone I'd forgotten, I was almost swept away by a rush of these angels, running home from school for the last time of the year, chanting

> No more spelling no more sums
> No more teachers to smack our . . .

At least that's what we used to chant, but though this had the same rhythm the words were different, and they were chanted so rapidly I couldn't catch them, which was horribly tantalising.

I went to a Christmas party for the children of the Children's Home whom I'd been used to see playing from my bedroom window. Here I still looked on, watched them downing enormous quantities of ice-cream and fizzy drink, and produce enormous amounts of breath to blow up balloons until they burst. I pulled crackers with them, and was quite unable to secure for myself the middle part of any of the crackers, and I despaired of getting a hat or a riddle, but I was always kindly given one. And then there was Father Christmas. I noticed an odd thing about Father Christmas, which must make him just about unique among entertainers, if you call him an entertainer; and this was that his audience decreased in proportion to the success of his act. When he arrived the whole audience watched every move he made and laughed at the little boy who was scared of him and laughed when he gave a comb to a man with a bald head and laughed at the little boy who wasn't scared of him; but as the presents came down one by one from the tree the audience turned one by one away from Father Christmas to winding up toys, chewing lollies, fondling dolls and reading books; and anything really spectacular, like a tricycle, would take the attention even of those whose turn was yet to come, even make them too preoccupied to hear their own names called. At the end of it Father Christmas crept away unnoticed by anyone.

After all this preliminary racket the day itself arrived very quietly, with no postman, no shopping, no rush. There was just staying in bed late, reading a book or two I'd been given, over-eating, sitting placidly on the veranda surrounded by family, talking, admiring the new twins, taking snaps of one another, admiring the garden, bouncing an occasional ball at an occasional child. The best of it was that it was such a relief to be getting away from Christmas. Unless, of course, this really was getting to Christmas.

Ten

I went exploring further. I saw bazaars and flower-shows. I watched a few polite overs being bowled on a suburban cricket ground and discovered for the first time, after years of listening to the commentaries on the wireless, that at the end of an over the players change over. I went to a wedding and to a funeral. I went to church services and enjoyed being one of a crowd of ordinary everyday sinners and hypocrites instead of hearing with half an ear their voices come out of a box by the bed. I went to a church tea and had too much to say at a discussion afterwards; and on the following morning heard from the surgeon, Mr R., who was visiting our town, what a risk I had run. 'The case history of one of our patients said he'd had his first bad attack after attending a church social. A clear case of guidance.'

And I went to the pictures.

Not to be able to go to the pictures is the sacrifice a person in bed must make which fit people seem to find most shocking, the thing they sympathise about most. I don't suppose they really believe films are of such first importance; but it's something direct and tangible by which they may grasp the meaning of being an invalid. And I thought of films in much the same way: films were a symbol of the world. I had always read the reviews and had sent my family to the films the critics thought most of, and when they came back they told me the plot. They told me: 'And after that she told him, at the head of the staircase, that she wasn't his great-aunt, she was his great-aunt's cousin – only I forgot to tell you that before this, on the day of the wedding, he'd murdered the butler, and that was why his great-aunt (only she was his great-aunt's cousin) decided to tell him the truth because then she had a hold on him.'

Relatives of invalids are the only people I know who can give away the plot of a film and be thanked for it, which may be some compensation for their hard lot otherwise.

To the pictures, then, was the first amusement I thought of going, and one of the first I did go to. My impression of the first film, however, was not exactly a first impression of films. As a child I had seen Shirley Temple and Sabu and Jane Withers and Errol Flynn as Robin Hood and *Snow White and the Seven Dwarfs* and *The Mutiny on the Bounty* and *Lorna Doone* and *The Count of Monte Cristo* – that one with the Abbé's head creeping through the hole in the wall, which still gives me the creeps to think of it. And a good many pictures besides these I remembered, and I remembered I would walk out of the picture thinking I was still in it, and the traffic and the street outside and my own movement through them took on a new look of mystery and romance until the effect wore off. But there had been years enough between to open my mind wide to any impressions that might care to present themselves.

The first impression was a headache; but thanks to aspirin it wasn't the most lasting. It's unnatural behaviour when you come to think of it, watching a changing intensity of flashing light on a screen for a couple of hours, watching it become enormous faces looming at you, mouthing words that boom at you with lips as big as your arm. And if I began to wonder whether the whole performance was any more natural, perhaps that was scarcely surprising since the film I was at was *Kind Hearts and Coronets,* which reversed most laws of probability, especially by showing Alec Guiness as all eight members of the noble d'Ascoyne family, including one woman, though a suffragette. But later films confirmed that my feeling of unreality in watching them did not depend on an unreal story. The reason was mostly that the picture came in the way of the story. I was too aware of seeing not events but a series of pictures of events. It seemed not created but contrived, contrived of little bits most skilfully put together, but so done that it was easier to watch the skill of the putting together than to penetrate that surface to see what the film was saying. It seemed remote, and a little cold: I found I was not now living in what I saw as once I had done, but watching it detached. I was finding myself aware – as I had naturally not been as a child – of the conventions a film depends on, of the amount it must deceive the viewer before he can believe its shadows are life; and I was finding a difficulty in being deceived that surprised me.

Then on top of this awareness of the illusion in film was a feeling that its realism was too real. *Kind Hearts and Coronets* was a satire; but the satire was only in its literary parts, the parts that existed before the film began to be made, and in the acting. Except in one or two minor sets and minor details in those sets the camera couldn't extend the satire to the scene it saw. The trees were nothing else than trees, nor castles than castles, nor churches than churches; indeed the greatest care seemed to have been taken to ensure that they should not be. Larger than life and quite as natural seemed to be the camera's motto; and this no doubt was why at times the camera could tell such convincing lies. (I saw newsreels too.) But there was always this conflict between the realism of the setting and the illusion by which it was conveyed. There soon were times when I began to feel inserted in a film but they didn't last long, and I felt less involved the faster or tenser the scene became, for then the screen seemed least adequate.

I had to recognise, then, that I had reservations about films, and I began to feel a traitor to the people who were glad because I could go to the pictures and to my own pleasure at being able to. I thought perhaps I had seen the wrong films, that as I saw more these limitations would disappear, that they might only appear to exist because I was not experienced enough in the medium to penetrate beyond them. But if so the necessary experience is taking a long time to acquire. Certainly I am less aware now than I was of particular conventions, my trouble with films tends to grow vague where it was explicit, but I fail yet to get much thrill from them. I enjoy going, I am entertained, but I seldom find myself genuinely moved or stirred.

This being my reaction to films I was surprised to find myself being fully satisfied by plays. I imagined that if pictures baffled me plays would baffle more. Their conventions surely demanded more of the audience. For this cockpit must hold the vasty fields of France and this wooden O the very casques that did affright the air at Agincourt. Whereas film, in appearance, was the muse of fire that would ascend the highest heaven of invention – a kingdom for a stage, princes to act. Yet the conventions which the stage required me to accept were so obvious it proved much easier to accept them and look beyond. In a film an appearance of reality hid the fact of unreality. In a play the unreal appearance could cloak something very nearly real; indeed it was real to the extent that the people were living people, not shadow. Certainly the plays I saw – the first three were by Shaw, Pirandello and Shakespeare – were all greater in themselves than any of the films, by any standard of judgment, even if the actors were not; which may have influenced my favourable impression. But I did not believe that was all there was to it. Not that I sat in the theatre analysing the thoughts and feelings the plays were producing. To me it seemed a miracle I was sharing in, and I sat enthralled and uncritical even through performances whose faults could wring columns of print from knowledgeable critics and which knowledgeable friends told me were not worth going to see. And why,

I wonder, did no one ever tell me what part colour and light play in a play?

Colour too was what first struck my ears when I went to a lunchtime concert by the National Orchestra – the colour of sound. I had learned to enjoy music from the radio, but to hear now an orchestra in the concert hall was like seeing the original of a painting I had long known in black-and-white: it suddenly took on new life and shade and stillness. The radio can give you music's form and some of its light and shade and there are possibly some kinds of music whose meaning appears adequately in their form, as there are some paintings whose colour is not important. But – though I admit I had never heard a really hi-fi instrument – I had not heard a radio which could convey adequately the brilliancies and mellownesses of tone, the loudness and the softness, the different expression of voice each instrument gives; I hadn't heard on the radio the real stringiness of strings, the real brassiness of brass; nor had I heard a radio which could both separate these elements and combine them again as my own ear could do as I sat there in the concert hall, helped no doubt by my eyes as they moved from instrument to instrument and appeared to guide the ear to pick up the sound each of them made. This I suppose was why, though Ravel's *Bolero* had always bored me on the radio, going on and on and on, I found myself almost jumping from my seat with excitement when I heard it at the concert. It isn't usual to hear unknown or esoteric works at a lunchtime concert. Some they played that day might be called hackneyed; but in its new setting it all seemed boundless with new sound. I sat and absorbed sound and found no time to think about what I was hearing at all.

That I did, nevertheless, find time to look at things while I was listening, and couldn't have helped looking if I had wanted to, was probably reprehensible. I had gathered that the proper attitude for a real music-lover when listening to music is with the head back and the eyes closed – or else with the head bent and the eyes fixed on a score. But my senses were not so independent that the pleasure of one had no effect on the pleasure of another. If music was less alive on the radio than in a hall it was partly perhaps because my eyes had then been either unoccupied or occupied with something quite irrelevant – with brushing my teeth, with a truck on the road; more usually with a book or a paper. Anyway I used my eyes shamelessly. To see, for instance, the audience; every one of whose enjoyment of the music added to everyone else's, increasing it collectively. The young man in the seat next to mine who read the murders in *Truth* between items and when the music began put it down and listened with all-absorbed concentration – and with his eyes closed. Or the office girls in front of me who sneaked sandwiches from boxes on their knees while they listened.

Then there was the conductor – it was Sir Bernard Heinze from Australia – who conducted with his whole body and being and never lost a hair out of its predestined place, except one, once, in one of the more passionate parts of Tchaikovsky's *Romeo and Juliet* overture. The leader who when he had a few bars rest took a piece of rosin from his waistcoat pocket, fiddled with it, put it back, fiddled with it. And the flautist who blew a note or two, wiped his mouth on the back of his hand, and blew another note or two. And the elderly upright cellist who picked up his bow and ran it over the strings and lowered it again quietly and fastidiously as one of the gentler counting-house clerks in Dickens might have wielded a quill pen. And the harpist, appearing and disappearing at her instrument like a wraith. And beyond all these the entire orchestra at its busier moments swaying and charging to one rhythm like a dance to emphasise the sound. I could not believe that this sight, at least, was irrelevant to the music. It reminded me that music began as a partner to the dance.

Eleven

I had now discovered objects and places from baths to ballet, but what I was increasingly discovering was the people who controlled and pervaded them all, the people who controlled and pervaded my experience of the world. The most important of the things I had discovered were people. This was not quite what I had expected: after all, people had been the part of the world I had most often seen when I had been away from the world. But people moved among and lived among were, I found, totally different creatures from people coming to visit an invalid. They were more various in their lives, more complex in their behaviour. There were, besides, many more of them.

It was the number of people which at first impressed me. I went, quite early in the piece, to see the Canterbury centennial procession and found the whole town gone with me, who lined the streets and rose from their verges like nasturtiums climbing a bank. I sat in the car – not yet being able to join a crowd anonymously – and watched, enjoying the procession but enthralled by this vast number of people. That each of these specks had its own unique life, its own thoughts and passions, was an idea the imagination could not begin to grasp.

When I went to town on more normal days I saw people in the streets on their daily business, hurrying along the pavements with grim and private faces. I saw them packed into a big city restaurant, bequeathing to their thousands of digestions whole barrow-loads of beef and potato and strawberry ices, and covering the agony with talk: quiet talk from each about maiden handicaps and the price of cretonne, that merged into a shriek of sound coming down from the ceiling hard upon the head. When I remembered there were people who ate in this atmosphere every day they worked, who lunched on fried sole with mashed potato and a slice of lemon every noon for years on end among all this clatter and roar, I could not wonder the mental hospitals were full.

Inevitably there were certain people who appeared more than once in these public places, and I was soon confronted by a friendly face looming out of the mass saying, 'Good afternoon, how are *you* today?' – a face I knew I knew; and I was sent into a panic trying to pin a name to it. And why all these people should insist on names of their own was a puzzle. You might as well name every sheep on a high country station.

Yet even when the mass crystallised into individuals they did not immediately become open and transparent. They still kept their real selves to themselves and confronted the curious with a mystery. I wandered about the streets watching people living their lives, trying to find out what they meant by it, failing to fit them into categories.

The telephone box around the corner had a vacant pane in it. How it had become vacant I never troubled to enquire. I found it that way when I first found the box and so it remained for a year or more afterwards, without even a jagged spike clinging to the frame. I passed it one day and saw a girl leaning through the gap, head in rump out, listening intently to the conversation a man was holding with the receiver. I wondered what she found so enthralling. I do not deliberately listen to other people's conversations: it is not polite; but, passing slowly by, I knew that if there was anything to hear I could not help hearing it. The girl still listened closely, so the voice was a little muffled by the barrier of flesh it had to pass through. I heard him clearly enough though, and what I heard was: 'I'll do the best I can for you as soon as possible.'

I passed on my way.

But at other times when I went about I heard an occasional passing phrase of conversation, a snatch of sound given me by no effort of my own, never to be found if I should make an effort, presented fortuitously, an unrehearsed revelation of what people were like. A boy passed me, saying to another boy: 'I'd like to be dowsed by King Neptune.' A girl passed me, saying to another girl: 'And all this happened because of a mistake in a telegram.'

An old man walked along the street wearing a spotless white topee, a spotless white beard, a spotless red waistcoat. He returned after a time, as I was talking to a friend on the telephone. I could see him clearly from the front hall. I described him.

'You are sure you can see him?' A. said.

I assured him I could.

'Too big for a gnome?'

I had reluctantly to admit he was too big for a gnome.

I saw a Bishop standing behind a shop counter animatedly discussing with an encompassing cloud of assistants a bale of purple cloth. I saw a woman walking past a petrol station dressed in a beautifully tailored suit with a silver fox fur, weeping beautifully into a white lace handkerchief, a stout party in grey at her side curving towards her voice a sympathetic ear.

I didn't know what to make of it all.

Conversation with people seemed to be used quite as often to conceal as to reveal. I would meet people with smiling private faces, we would pat a customary ball of conversation back and forth; about the weather, about the age and health of their canary or their cat, about the habits of ants; fumbling a little now and then if the partners were not well known, but on the whole keeping up the game tolerably well; and neither side allowing any inkling of their real selves to break up the party. I would sit in on an afternoon tea. One of us would talk about pumpkins; another of us would talk about cauliflowers. Or Mrs B. would tell us how she loved England.

'We all love England,' she said, 'we call England Home.'

Mrs C. said she loved Cicely Courtneidge. We all loved Cicely Courtneidge, we all said.

'I think Gracie Fields' marriage is a mistake,' Mrs B. said; 'but they write dreadful things in the sensational papers, like the *Auckland Star*.'

'I love the English papers,' Mrs C. said.

Sometimes I thought I couldn't fathom folk, and sometimes I wondered if there was anything to fathom. I learned from our novelists and short story writers that there was indeed something to fathom: anguish. But even this kept itself hid.

What I did begin to find beneath the surface was a variety of ways of living and especially of working which was quite strange. I would watch from a distance people doing things entirely different from anything I had ever done myself or could ever hope to do: men stripped to a warm day stacking sacks of grain or timber on a wharf, working with their bodies in a way I never knew from my own experience bodies could be worked, heaving, swaying with a casual confident strength; while the neatly clothed bodies of clerks tripped among them, divided by their looks into another species.

I watched a tree doctor doctoring a tree. 'Nature doesn't always make a very good job of a tree, but art can do it for her,' he said, and he sat drinking his morning tea and talked about trees, identifying several I did not know with the confident assurance of the expert. (And the next tree expert I met as confidently contradicted all the identifications.) I watched two men, one young, one older, one called Mick, the other called Mac, installing a refrigerator; and appearing to have a complete understanding not only of the refrigerator but also of themselves installing a refrigerator. I saw a man wrapping apples at an orchard, burying them in tissue paper, laying them in boxes, so deftly and rapidly, with such sleight of hand, that you couldn't see the detail of how it was done. I saw a postman sorting mail outside our gate on a frosty morning, who told me that frost made his hands so numb he couldn't feel to separate the letters efficiently. He laid out a row of individually addressed catalogues from a mailorder firm. '*This* is what we like,' he said, meaning he didn't. I heard from a chimney-sweep the subtle tricks of sweeping chimneys.

Even people who did work I could with a little stretch of the imagination think myself capable of doing revealed extraordinary powers when I saw them at work; working in crowded offices with desks pushed against each other, with people walking in and out, telephones ringing, typewriters clattering, and yet managing to get through work which needed considerable concentration.

All these people knew, or seemed to know, exactly what they needed to know; while I was finding more and more how little I knew which everyone else took for granted. As I stood at the gate one day a small boy came along the street wheeling a bicycle. Seeing with sudden relief a man, or what he took to be a man, he wheeled his bicycle across and asked if I could mend his broken chain. I had to confess I hadn't the faintest idea how to mend his broken chain. He seemed scarcely to believe it. Absurdly simple things had me baffled. A relative I was staying with went to town one day and left me with the job of feeding the cat. 'Cut the meat into little pieces,' she said. In due course the cat came in, squeaking. I took the saucer of meat from the safe and began hacking at it with a tableknife while it was still on the saucer. Every time I stroked it with the knife it merely gave way and then sprang back into place like a fiendish piece of india-rubber. I hacked at it until I was soaked in sweat, my wrist was aching, and the cat nearly demented. I tried the carving knife and got on little better. Then suddenly, from some remote part of my mind there popped into consciousness a suspicion that I had seen meat being cut up on a wooden board. I found such a board, and the cat was soon appeased.

What I found was that familiarity with loading ships, topping trees, chopping cats-meat, gave a person a whole new life, not only to his body but to his mind. He spoke an entirely different language. It was not always very articulate, but I had pleasure in hearing people talk of what they did, if they would. I began to pick up some of the peculiar jargon of occupations, pretending to understand what I was told about ryegrass and red clover, two-tooth ewes and crutching; about brake horsepower and overhead valves and apertures and exposures and ems and points and beards. I might even try to talk about them, but this usually led to my receiving the same sort of look I got when I talked about art to people who knew about art. It was all so new that even the bore failed to bore and I was far too interested in everyone to be able to dislike anyone. But all things come in time.

Yet in all these new experiences I was still from long usage looking and listening from a distance, detached. It was not the looking and the listening, it was the amount I now began to be involved with people, that measured my entry into the world. Then I saw people grow even more new parts and powers at the same time as I was aware of the same growing in myself. During those years in bed my family had to do most of my work with the world and be those parts of myself I was unable to be. And if I asked one of them to buy some stamps and I worked the sum wrong and sent the wrong money (which frequently happened) and the Post Office clerk's eyebrows rose up; or if another of my relatives had to tramp half-a-dozen stores to get my kind of pyjamas – I heard of these adventures certainly, but that wasn't the same as being in them. Then I got up and the family thankfully handed over these functions to me, in gentle stages, and I had to grow new functions like new limbs. I found I was a feeble fool and putty and butter and everything that didn't know its own mind.

There was the day I went to buy some clothes – a good many clothes because I didn't feel up to wearing pyjamas to the pictures. 'Now I want you to take just what you like best,' the salesman said, and I carried away all the clothes the salesman liked best. And then one day I walked to the store – very proud of walking to the store – and forgetting about inflation asked for a *sixpenny* block of ice-cream. The woman was very kind, certainly. And I got into a contretemps at a bookshop where I handed some books to the girl at a counter – the wrong girl, as it happened, and the wrong counter.

'Do you want these credited to your account?' she asked.

The account was very new and I wasn't thinking very hard.

'Yes,' I said; 'but don't bother to wrap them up,' I added kindly.

'Do you want to take them with you?' she wanted to know, incredulously.

I was puzzled to think why I shouldn't, and we stood looking at one another for a couple of minutes until a senior assistant came to our rescue and suggested I wanted them charged to my account.

Another day I went into a stationers' and asked for a ream of typing paper.

'Yes?' said the brisk assistant. 'Eighteen pounds? Twenty pounds?' I was appalled. I thought she meant the price.

These encounters made me aware of something I had never suspected: that I was absent-minded. I had always considered myself a rational, collected person, especially when I was telling other people what to do; but under the stress of doing them for myself I fumbled, I forgot to pay for my purchases, I left without my change, or I dropped it on the floor when I thought I was putting it in my pocket. It was a new experience to have to consider myself a fool.

I did in time become a little more used to the ways of the world; but I also realised I was not now more independent than I once was, I was merely dependent on many more people. My awareness of my dependence on my family before had concealed my, and their, dependence on everyone else. I now began to grasp how closely and inevitably and with what complexity each person is related to each other person.

With what complexity. People depended on each other without being like each other. Their lives had patterns as infinitely various as their fingerprints. Some people felt more active in the morning, some at night; some preferred to sit in the sun and some in the shade; some liked to wash and some to dry; some poured milk into the cup before the tea and some after. Going among people I came with a bump against these idiosyncrasies which had so surprisingly to be taken into account before I could live comfortably with people; idiosyncrasies I regarded with irritation or pity or amused tolerance, and which they seemed to think unaccountably important. People, I found, were queer. And then I found that my own logical, reasonable, entirely sane routine of life these people regarded as my idiosyncrasy, with irritation or pity or amused tolerance. If people were queer, it seemed, I was queer. People were their idiosyncrasies.

And yet they could not live separate, unmeeting, unattached lives, however much some of them might wish to. The whole art of dealing with people consisted in rotating together square pegs and round holes without producing sparks. My experience of regaining the world was not merely a matter of being able to move where once I was still, of being able to go around corners where once I could see only in a straight line. It was that when I moved away from my former fixed position I began to feel as the contemporaries of Copernicus and Galileo must have felt when they were told – and refused to believe – that the earth was not the centre of the universe. I might still believe – most people do believe that I really was still the centre of my world; but I had to recognise it was a moving centre, moving in a complicated orbit among a lot of other bodies which were all convinced they were the centre of the world, and I had to move among them without colliding.

Once every person I saw came to *me* through the door to *my* room and interrupted *my* progress of time. And this expressed more than the physical fact of their coming and going. People do accommodate themselves to an invalid. They put themselves out, and try to avoid putting him out. They make few demands on him, and thus conceal from him the demands he is making on them. But now that I was out in the world, joining in its life, I was able to see that even for so simple an arrangement as a group of people coming together, converging, to a meeting or a lunch, they must each adjust their own progress of time and life, they must each alter slightly their usual habits, and spend endless time consulting and telephoning, working out how to do it; and for each engagement altered to make room for this new one, somebody else's routine must be affected, and they in turn must affect other people, a wave advancing in a mathematical progression which must soon threaten to reach the whole world. So for half-a-dozen people to meet over a cup of tea, the world must move over to make room. It was difficult enough when everyone was willing to meet; when they were not and had to be persuaded; or even if they were but were absent-minded or so attached to their regular habits that it was an effort to them to move from them, whole new complications arose. And when these complications threatened to arise, and they usually did, not over a mere meeting of people but over some matter of much more importance, and I had to try to sort them out, I began to feel like a description I read in a book of the *Inadequate Psychotic.*

Yet a complete failure of plans does not perhaps worry a former invalid as much as a person who has been accustomed to have everything go right. An invalid has been used to things going wrong, to having hopes disappointed, and fears also often enough; and for a time at least he carries over into his active life a protecting felt around the mind which prevents his self from being too heavily penetrated either by disappointment or by fulfilment, even when he wants it to be. But I must admit that when for the first time or two plans I had made were frustrated not by my own illness but by somebody else's – nothing serious of course, just a mild attack of flu – I took a shameful pleasure in the fact. And I had a degrading suspicion that the enjoyment I had in visiting people in hospital was not merely kindly or altruistic. I meant no harm to the person who was in bed, but it was – well, satisfactory, to be the one who was out of it.

Twelve

During those years in bed I had read the works of New Zealand writers, I had heard them on the radio, I had looked at pictures of them when I could find them. I had watched them quarrelling in the correspondence columns of the *Listener*, I had extracted news of them from anyone I met who might know them, until I was almost persuaded I knew them myself and had some difficulty in restraining myself from talking as if I did. Now it seemed I might have some chance of really meeting a few.

In 1951 a Writers' Conference was held in Christchurch, celebrating (though in what way did not seem very clear) the Canterbury centennial. It was open to the public and a clergyman I knew invited me to go with him to one of the sessions. Which one, we decided more from our own convenience than because we knew who was speaking, but we chose well. It was a frosty morning, a grey soft misty morning, the streets deep in fallen leaves, when we arrived at Canterbury College and made our way to the lecture room. We were the first to arrive except for a radio technician who was sending incomprehensible messages back along the wire to the studio. We climbed scrupulously past the first layer of seats, marked *Professors,* and past the next two or three layers, marked *Writers,* and sat half-way up. Then the conference proper, who had evidently collected at some assembly point outside, trooped in together. Professors climbed up to our level, some of the Writers even higher, leaving the front seats for the aged and infirm. I was busy scanning faces as their owners swarmed to their seats, lit cigarettes, poked the ashes into the inkwells, busy noting their dressing, which had reacted against convention with such unanimity that they looked collectively queer but individually uniformed. I darted my eyes from one to another, comparing features with photographs retained in the memory, trying to identify them. This spectacled person almost lost in an immense cloaking yellow hooded greatcoat, no doubt picked up on his recent trip abroad; yes, I knew who *he* was. The three bowed white heads two rows below me – I knew who two of them belonged to, though the third eluded me; these two even older heads tottering in on exhausted legs, no trouble at all; nor that moustache. The younger men, whose features had not been so often publicised, nor for so long, were more elusive and required more tentative labelling, most of which I later found to have been mistaken. The man with the black pointed beard who wrote busily in a notebook just under my chin, the very young man whose grubby white corduroy slacks brushed against my right ear – I don't yet know who they really were. But there was no doubt about the identity of this other young man in a blue pullover with a slight stoop and a brooding eye, the poet who looked like a poet: he was the speaker for the morning. When he began to speak, reading from a script, slowly, beautifully, quoting poems (and he pronounced the words poem, poet and poetry in a rich rounded fashion which made tangible his belief in them), his audience all realised they were present at an occasion. I watched their absorption as they listened, heard the respectful laughter at a joke now and then, saw the rigidly unexpressive faces of poets when he talked of them.

When he had finished, my clerical companion turned to me and said, 'What a fine sermon!' The conference retired to the Students'

Union for morning tea, but that was too far yet for me to walk, so I stayed where I was, talking to my friend about the state of the world.

'Now tell me, Dennis,' he said, 'where are we all going? Are we going anywhere? Can you tell me?'

Only two other people stayed in the hall, two old ladies, one of whom said a piece of poetry slowly into her friend's ear which her friend repeated and savoured. I had not by then much stamina for these events and began to feel tired, so I did not wait for the discussion which followed. As the writers began filing back I left, having seen writers, having been near writers, even if I hadn't met them, yet feeling I was getting near that world. It was one of the happiest mornings I could remember.

What I now wanted to do was to meet a few of these people whose faces I had seen for a moment. I wanted to go lion-hunting. But I was inhibited by good manners: I couldn't bring myself to write to any of them and say hey I want to meet you, when can I come. I had to wait until I found somebody who knew somebody and was willing to perform the necessary introductions. Opportunities came in time: the first from the editor of the *Outlook*. I went with him and my parents and his family in our car around the Port Hills to a small farm in one of the valleys, the editor of the *Outlook* complaining the whole way that he would rather be riding his bicycle. We went to visit the rural sage who wrote every week in one of the weekly papers, a large, square, white-haired man in a Norfolk jacket, who met us with his dog Mac, his cow Elsie, with blossoms on the apple trees, and under the apple trees the lambs of whom he had been wondering in print a week or two before whether they should be tailed with the knife or by constriction. He and his attractive wife led us into their living-room where there was a fire, and varnished walls almost entirely concealed by books, thousands of books of every kind that demands to be read, and we sat there and talked – listened, much of the time, to him talking.

And talk, I discovered, was the magic of lion-hunting; that, and the fact that I was no longer exhausted after only half-an-hour of it. The talk was on all kinds of topics – I don't know what wasn't talked about. The quiz-kids, the money-raising methods of the late Mr Ell who built the Sign of the Takahe and the Summit Road, vandalism, journalistic ethics and the politics of the *New Zealand Herald,* the farmer whose child suffered from eczema until he fed her on goats' milk, after which, 'there isn't a lovelier kid in the district,' he said. But it didn't really matter what he talked about: his talk was what mattered, talk informed by a lifetime of living and thinking, and brought out quite ungrudgingly to entertain a casual stranger.

The next writer I met was an Auckland novelist who had once been shown one of my stories by my friends in Bayswater and had liked it and helped me get it published, and whom I now approached with a good deal of diffidence. I visited him in his little house where he sat perched on a high stool at the sort of counter which separated the sitting from the kitchen part of his living-room, on which there was a chess-board, and rows of tomatoes and green and red peppers from his garden. The garden surrounded the house and asserted a place for the Wilderness in the midst of the City – a fruitful wilderness, too, as the tomatoes and peppers showed, as well as his own conversation. He was looked down on by a Keith Patterson cat. He showed no resentment that I had interrupted his work. He received me graciously, kindly, courteously, sat me down, and began to talk, showing a depth of erudition on a range of topics that amazed me, who had perhaps judged how he would talk from the apparently more elemental characters in his stories; on a wider range of topics than it would occur to most of our intellectuals even to think about. Only occasionally, beneath the talk of theology, which changed to a speculation about why his chinese gooseberries should suddenly have fruited for the first time for years, and back again to golden boughery, did I detect a sign of the observant eye of an analyst summing up a case. He asked about my operation, and then turned by chance steps which it would be difficult to retrace to Mr Hoyle's theories of the universe.

'I like the way,' he said, 'he calmly tells us that at a certain date a few million years hence the seas will dry up and then the rocks will begin to boil, and the sun will expand to envelop the earth. Though mind you, it's a great triumph for the church.'

'The medieval pictures not so far off after all?'

'There's one part of the medieval cosmology I regret, though. That crystal firmament just above your head. Very comforting.'

I fervently agreed. Mr Hoyle made me giddy. Then he told me about the latest of the lame dogs he seemed always to be keeping an eye on. And about Proust – 'who decided that being an invalid was his vocation' – and back to my operation, and wondering if it were a good thing to interfere with *my* natural vocation. An explosion of laughter. But kindly, interested; conveying the impression – which was certainly a delusion – that at that moment at least I was the only person who mattered. I went home enchanted, full of enough conversation to last me for weeks, a character to try to fathom, and a certainty that when I thought I had done so I would still be a long way wide of the mark.

I also met a poet, who didn't look like a poet, and who talked mostly about juvenile delinquency; and his wife, who, when I talked with praise of the poet's poetry, looked sardonic.

And, since there are more critics of New Zealand writing than there are New Zealand writers, I also met several critics. On one memorable occasion I spent several hours, on two successive days, with a critic from each side of the current literary schism. I did not have them *together,* but one at a time. They had, I believe, been together an evening or two before, and I wished I had been there then. Or maybe I didn't. I found it hard enough to keep my balance as it was. It was clear enough that there was just then a sharp division into two factions, but the nature of the factions and of their beliefs was less easy to discover. Some said they were the old versus the young, but in this pair the up-and-coming youngster was a year older than the old fogey. Some said they were the academics and the anti-academics. This was more satisfactory. My academic critic certainly lectured at the university. So, as it happened, did the other, but not in the English department, which, it seemed, was a sign of grace. When I made a closer effort to discover the principles each stood for, I found I got the most cogent account of each from his opponent, so the picture which began to emerge may have been a little misleading. The academic critics, it seemed, sat in their studies casting a cold eye over the poets' work, blue-pencilling an incongruity here, a far-fetched image there, refusing to accept anything but what they had previously been used to reading, comparing new poets to old and finding them wanting, and generally perceiving with a fine discrimination everything but the essential spirit of the poem. But according to the same academic critics this picture was composed by poets who resented on principle being criticised at all. The new critics, on the other hand, with Freud in one pocket and Margaret Mead in the other, were engaged in elucidating from the works of the new poets and prose-writers an exploration of the national neurosis: 'and to explore the national neurosis in any but sexual terms,' my academic critic explained to me, 'is not literature, but preaching.' The new critics were favoured by the new poets because they favoured the new poets, but the poets seemed not entirely willing, all the same, to turn themselves wholly into cultural anthropologists and continued serenely along their own paths. It was confusing altogether, however lucid it might appear to my two critics.

Both of them had the talent to have been actors, if their brains hadn't got in the way. One of them read aloud poems he did not admire, and made a burlesque of them (he was selecting an anthology); the other delicately mimicked people's way of talking. They both talked brilliantly; while I concentrated on concealing as well as I could what I did not know, and on keeping from expressing any definite opinion at all. To save myself from becoming the target of their intellectual big guns – not that I would have done, probably, for they both had kind natures, towards me at least: but I knew what they would be thinking behind their smiles – I gave each the hypocritical impression that I was entirely on his side. Or perhaps not entirely hypocritical, since I thought in my undoubted ignorance there was a lot to be said on both sides; and to the best of my ability I let each of them see by an appropriate nod here and there what I thought was to be said on his side and charitably left out any qualifications. But to the one to whom I confessed a liking for the poetry of Ursula Bethell I could not mention that I also liked the poetry of Louis Johnson, and to the other I had to be discreet in reverse. I did not tell them that what I most enjoyed was sitting back and watching the fight – though perhaps the fight was what they most enjoyed too, not to mention the poets. And I admired the intellect of each, which was capable at a moment's notice of thinking up arguments I couldn't have thought of in several years.

And besides their brains I liked themselves: I liked the diarist and the novelist and the poet and the critics; I liked them especially for the friendly way they put up with me, when there certainly was no reason why they should. Whether, in fact, they gave themselves to me any more than most people did, I couldn't say; but even after protecting their inner core they had enough over for me not to notice where, in fact, they drew the line.

A few other people of the kind I have met for a moment at decorous literary evenings where the guests moved around trying to buttonhole somebody, who, as soon as they had succeeded, was purloined by somebody else; or where everybody stayed put in their chairs, sipping drinks, nibbling peanuts and potato-chips, segregating themselves inevitably according to their sex, although they will write diatribes in public against this habit.

'We ought to be trying to break this up,' said a guest at one such party, when he saw the women rising to one end of the room while the men settled to the other.

'It is difficult to break up the social pattern,' said another.

'Especially when the social pattern is sitting down,' said the first.

And the talk blows about with the tobacco-smoke as people attach their voices to one group or to another, keeping an ear on concurrent conversations for fear they are missing something; and different conversations coalesce for a moment and then break up into fragments again. Such affairs can be entertaining; but successful lion-hunting needs to be tête-à-tête, or nearly so.

That I began after a time to do more than merely listen to other people who wrote was a consequence of writing a rash letter to the talks officer of the local radio station congratulating him on one of his programmes. When he replied he suggested, on spec evidently, that I might do a programme for him about beards. Why *beards*? I didn't know; nor did I know anything about beards; but I suggested instead some talks about regaining the world. He said okay, and I set to work on the first talk of a series which was to be the basis of this book.

When I let him know I had done it he visited me to hear it read: a tall broad man with a piratical black eyeshade over one eye and an R.A.F. upbringing. He called me old boy. He sat drinking tea and eating a pavlova, which my mother had made to help towards a good impression, while I read the script. When I had finished he said he liked it.

'Though you read too quickly,' he said; 'you'll have to do a lot of practice before you record. You want to sit and read it to a vase to get the idea of talking to an object.'

These words terrified me. I had not the faintest desire to record the talks myself. I was sure I could never do it, and I tried to persuade him to get a professional to read them. He wouldn't hear of it. 'You wrote it,' he said, 'and no one else can give it the stresses you intend. The professionals elocute.' So I found I had let myself in for more than I intended.

He told me something about his job. 'The amount of letter-writing and form-filling you must do to get out a fifteen-minute talk,' he said, 'is incredible. But head office is very good. If you want to produce a series of 156 talks on breeding tropical fish they'll let you, though no one will listen to them.'

He said a few words about a literary problem he was engaged in puzzling out: namely, who killed Beth March? He expressed the opinion that it was Jo, with arsenic, and that their father was a dipsomaniac. To which I added my own literary speculation: was Paul Dombey a blue-baby? And he left me to write the other three talks.

While I was sweating them out on to old Christmas cards, and throwing card after card into the wastepaper basket, I was also getting the jitters about recording them. I woke on the morning with a sore throat – psychosomatic is the word for it, I believe. I sucked lozenges and my voice did not disappear as I had half hoped it would. The talks officer, wishing to spare me exertion, had insisted I should not come to the studio. He would bring a technician and a tape-recorder to the house. I somehow managed to survive the morning until they arrived; they set up their traps, sat me in front of the microphone – which, to make it the right height, was propped on several volumes of the *Historians' History of the World* (24 vols., 1908) – and disappeared, leaving me with the object which in anticipation had reduced me to such a jelly, confronted by it, staring at it. Then we were off. Fortunately I had read and re-read the script to a Satsuma vase until I had it almost by heart, so that even when the mind abdicated in terror the tongue babbled on. And after the first two or three paragraphs I found I was enjoying it. It was a curious experience. There I was all by myself putting on an act in front of a cold inanimate piece of metal which gave no sign at all of having heard a word. Even my best jokes passed it by without the slightest intensification of the blue metallic glitter which showed through the grating. My breath held out, too, better than I had hoped it would, although I had to group my words with shorter intervals between breaths than most people needed to do. My mother had been sitting the whole time over the telephone to suppress it at once if it should ring, but fortunately it didn't, though the tape did pick up a passing train.

When I had finished my piece the talks man popped back into the room looking at his stop-watch; and suddenly I heard a high-pitched voice echoing the words I had just been reading, the voice of a stranger, yet keeping faithfully to my own interpretation of my words. I had been warned beforehand that one's own voice sounds to oneself nothing like what it does to other people, with explanations about the distorting effect of head-bones and the inner ear; but even so it was some moments before I could grasp that this voice was my own. I could not associate it with myself at all. But my astonishment at it was not so great as my astonishment that neither the talks officer nor my mother was astonished at it at all. Unbelievable as it seemed, this was apparently what they expected me to sound like. To be quite honest I was not at that moment dissatisfied with the voice I heard; it was only later, when I had heard it more often and had almost succeeded in associating it with myself, as a person who has had his face remodelled must eventually do after looking often in the mirror, that I came to loathe it more and more. It was the kind of voice that belonged to the kind of person I most disliked. And when in due course my friends heard this voice coming from the radios they told me I sounded just as if I were in the room with them. And they remarked how calm, how relaxed I was.

Meanwhile I had recorded the second talk and was to have a few days' rest before doing the last two. The technician had packed his bags and on his way out told me he thought they were good talks. I had a high opinion of the intelligence of radio technicians from then on.

Later I advanced to recording at the studio and got to know that routine. There was the making of an appointment as if one were visiting a dentist (and I was not sure at first which experience was the more pleasant), the waiting in the lobby until the clock came round to the appointed time, clutching the script, which was crumpled from the amount of rehearsing needed to make it sound spontaneous, watching people scurry out of doors and into other doors carrying slips of yellow or blue paper or piles of records, watching the girl on the telephone switchboard casually plug into Auckland or Dunedin and take a second off to tell an anxious local caller the time. And then there was the studio with the dead echoless atmosphere which hits you as you pass through the heavy baize-covered door; there was the carafe and glasses which I didn't have the courage to touch in case it wasn't meant for me; the enclosed, cut-off feeling, when the baize-covered door was closed and I was alone, able to communicate only by means of red lights and loudspeaker; and yet through the double glass panels the technician was keeping a calm eye and finger on half-a-dozen processes at once and chatting with a casual caller with noiseless lips, while I was trying to keep my eye on my script.

I have also watched other people record and have seen the disc revolving slowly and throwing off its hair-threads of swarf, which are swept aside by a little brush, and the dial measuring the volume of the voice in decibels, which, while the cutter is turning the voice into grooves on wax, turns it into the flicker of a needle, suiting the action to the words with uncanny precision.

This was not the world regained: it was part of a new world I had never expected to gain. Yet though it was enjoyable, and it was satisfactory to be earning an honest penny from it, I had a few pangs of conscience at the thought that I was adding another voice to the babel with which we have learned to drug ourselves, which even when we think we are educating ourselves by listening to scholarly talks on Archaeology in Central Asia or the Structure of the Personality, are lulling us into a fond state where we comfortably exchange the necessity to live for hearing how others live. But I accepted the fact that you cannot expect to retain your innocence intact when you let yourself into the world, I continue to talk on the radio as often as they will let me, and be damned to conscience.

Thirteen

I enjoyed going for holidays. I felt I had all the holidays I had missed to make up; and for several years grew restless to be away from home every few months, even if it were just for a few days in a boarding-house at some holiday resort not far away. Old boarding-houses, most of them, with confusing corridors, with floors that had developed a list from north to south, and settled painfully to their most comfortable extension during the night, to be awoken with loud groans by the first foot that walked on them in the morning. They had temperamental doors, windows that rattled in the wind, and (in one place) a lavatory pan whose inside was beautifully stencilled with larger than life coloured carnations. The walls were far from soundproof and admitted the whole conversation of the family in the next room. I would lie on my bed wishing they would talk about something interesting, something scandalous; but they would obstinately persist throughout the time when all sane holidaymakers siesta in discussing the direction of north or the state of the roads hereabouts, comparing them with the roads where they came from and the direction of north where they came from; giving themselves a snack at 2.30 because it was not provided by the management.

'Would you like some cape gooseberry jam, Dad? Do you like cape gooseberry?'

'I'll eat anything my dear. Turnips would do.'

'Ah, well, it makes a change.'

Sounds which lulled me after a few days into a torpor from which I was unable any longer to distinguish individual words; and it was just at this blessed point that they would run across their cousin Nellie, an enormous woman who quivered about the town in a bright floral blouse and blue shorts. They did not like Cousin Nellie and enlarged on the reasons why, but by that time I could no longer hear what they said, even by listening hard.

At the table everyone soon knew the names and business of everyone else; the teachers who were there because they had to be; the elderly people who stayed there, sometimes lived there, because they liked it; the honeymoon couples taking in the scenery, photographing themselves against it for an album to look fondly back on, while attending to the rest of the business which had brought them there.

There was an old lady who arrived in a taxi from Christchurch, attended by her housekeeper. Her memory had entirely gone. She was fond of her food and sat in the lounge all morning, patiently waiting for lunch. She enjoyed eating it, but as soon as she had finished forgot she'd had it.

'Will it soon be time for lunch?' she would ask.

'You have had your lunch,' her housekeeper reminded her.

'Of course I have,' she would say, striving to remember; and with no memory of meals in the past, only a hope for a meal in the future, she would settle down patiently to wait for her dinner. Every morning she stood on the veranda and pointed across the bay.

'Did you ever hear,' she would ask anyone who happened to be by, 'about the dreadful tragedy that happened over there?'

New faces would appear at table, faces as withdrawn and remote as one's own had been the first evening, faces which would be filled out and animated by casual exchanges over the salt cellars during the next few days.

I liked to read the local paper if there was one where I stayed; I liked to see its prose style – to see whether it was written by someone to whom English came hardly and played tricks with the sense he wished to convey, or whether the reporter was an old-fashioned stylist ('an atmosphere of cordial conviviality was in abundant evidence at the Fire Brigade social last week'), or whether he read *Time*. Residents could not understand this interest. 'You don't want to *read* our rag, do you? There's never anything in it'; while I was being amazed at how much there was in it. A serial story, an article on Henry Sewell's diary, another by the Vicar on Muslim beliefs regarding the last day; not to mention reports from the Women's Institute, the golf club, the cricket club and Federated Farmers. I liked poking around the little shops, and in one stationer's found among the tiny stock of books which consisted almost entirely of Enid Blyton and Peter Cheyney, a copy of James Joyce's *Ulysses*. I wondered if he knew too little about it, or too much.

When I went further afield I travelled at first mainly by air, more because it got me there quickly than because I liked it better than any other way. I had of course travelled by air before so I hadn't the new discoveries to make now which startle you when you do it first – the lack of any great sensation of speed, the turning of the ground below into the similitude of those toy farmyards I used to gaze at in Whitcombe's when I was small, until you rise higher when it becomes more like a relief map. But I had more energy to notice. I grew used to the routine of going, of getting the seat numbers, of sitting about waiting, of boarding and fastening the belts while the plane did its preliminary tugging at the leash as the engines went through their regulation revolutions before we were finally off. It was a routine which was identical at all the airports, which were themselves as alike as the routine, so that on a long trip calling at several places I began to feel like the elderly Cook's tourist in Du Maurier's cartoon:

'And where, may I ask, are you going next?'

Right: Douglas Robb's wife Helen and children John, Jenny and Sarah meet him on his return from studying heart surgery in the United States, July 1948
ROBB COLLECTION, UNIVERSITY OF AUCKLAND LIBRARY

Below: A heart operation at Green Lane, 1951. The surgeons from left are Douglas Robb, Rowan Nicks (Mr N.), and Gordon Murray, a visiting surgeon from Canada

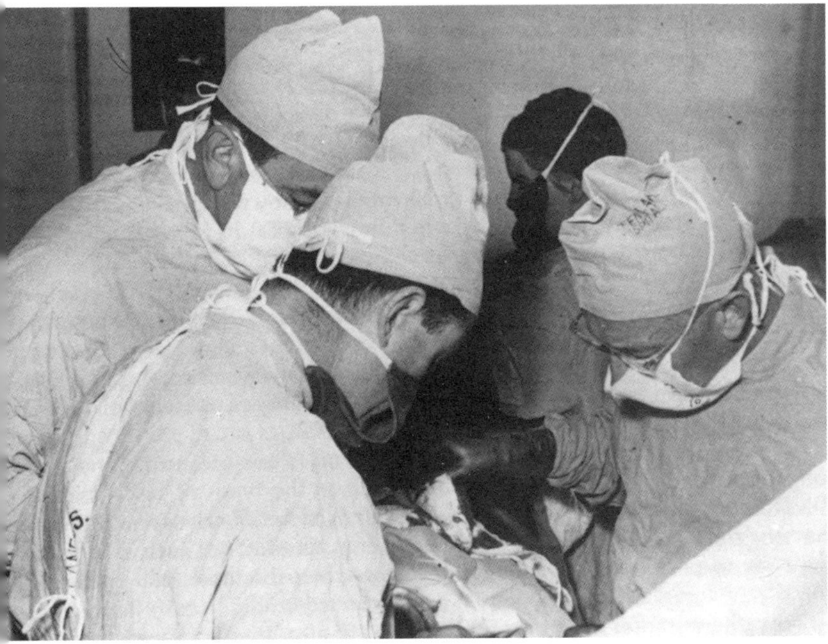

Above: 'A sliding diaphragmatic hernia.' Russell Clark's (imaginary) illustration for a short story based on my Green Lane experience
NEW ZEALAND LISTENER

Left: 'Blue-babies were still news.' While I was in Auckland my cousin John photographed this float in the Canterbury College capping procession

The sky was finally conquered – on Paekakariki Hill

With Christmas Greetings

from

* *Richard Dennis McEldowney*

9 Windermere Road
Papanui
Christchurch N.W.2

* *Delete name not required*

Left: The card for the first Christmas out of hospital (printed by the Caxton Press) had to cater for those in the hospital who knew me as Richard and those outside who didn't

Below: Zoe Greenhough, later my wife, sits in the chair with the two red wooden wheels

Right: 'A Christmas party for the children of the Children's Home next door'

Below: 'The enthusiastic Miss J.' (Muriel Johnston) with a friendly neighbourhood dog.
COURTESY PETER MURRAY

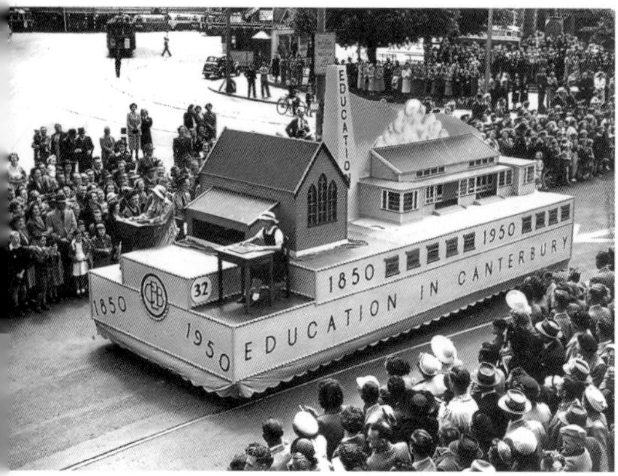

Left: 'You might as well name every sheep on a high country station.' 'Vast' crowds watch the Canterbury Centennial Procession, 18 December 1950
PRESS PHOTOGRAPH

Below: The rural sage: Oliver Duff, first editor of the *New Zealand Listener* ROBIN SMITH

Above: 'With a slight stoop and a brooding eye, the poet who looked like a poet.' James K. Baxter (fifth from left) at the 1951 Writers' Conference JAMES KEIR BAXTER COLLECTION, ALEXANDER TURNBULL LIBRARY, F-31258-1/2. PHOTO W. MCKASKELL, COURTESY NORMA MCKASKELL

Left: 'I went to a wedding', and the bride grabbed me for a photograph

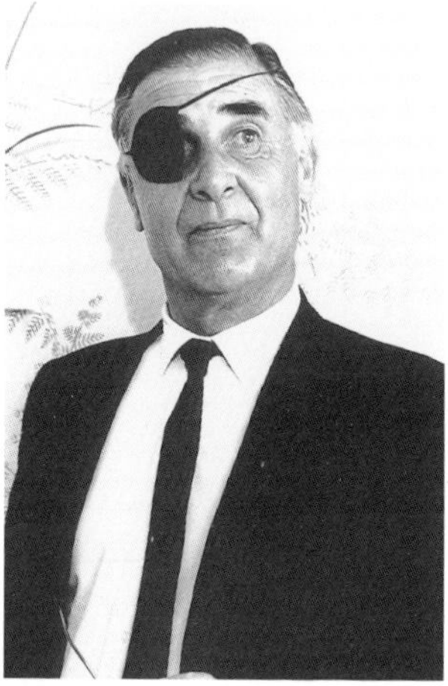

Above: The Auckland novelist:
Frank Sargeson in my aunt's window

Right: 'With a piratical black eyeshade':
Arnold Wall COURTESY MATTIE WALL

Below: Upper Hutt Library, up stairs behind
shops. Among the volunteers from right,
May O'Leary, Margaret Robertson,
Margaret McEldowney

'Oh! let me see – I'm going to Geneva!'

'*Going* to Geneva! Why, you *are* in Geneva!'

'Am I really? Oh, then I'm going to Milan!'

I was grateful for any incident that would fix a place in my mind as distinct from any other place. I remember Napier by a dignified white-moustached gentleman who, returning to the plane after the brief stop, stooped between the seats and came up dangling on his forefinger a very small, blue, knitted doll's beret.

'Dear me,' said the gentleman, 'someone will be wanting this,' and he called from the door of the plane for the bus to be delayed.

'Well fielded, sir!' he cried as he bowled the hat into the hands of an oncoming passenger, who handed it to an airways' official, who sidled up to the bus with it, obviously wishing he were somewhere else.

The people who travelled by air were almost as alike as the airports they flew from and the planes they flew in, well-dressed and anonymous, the men carrying despatch cases, with a sprinkling of the elderly and infirm who were fussed aboard by the hostesses who had once fussed me aboard. But now and then the uniformity was broken. My mother and I once travelled from New Plymouth to Wellington in a plane which was almost filled by white-moustached gentlemen, all of them obviously travelling by air for the first time and as excited about it as children. One of them, handing Minties around, told my mother they were going to a South African War Veterans' conference in Nelson. My mother, a little untactfully perhaps, asked him:

'How many of you are there to gather now?'

'I don't know,' he said cheerfully, 'but a hundred and fifty of us died last year.'

On another journey I sat across the aisle from a famous Chinese singer and his wife who spent the time looking through a nicely bound scrapbook of press-clippings of their New Zealand tour. And I remember two women. One was a nun, travelling alone, which made me think she could not belong to a Catholic order – yet she wore all the accoutrements, including a rosary. She was a sweet-faced girl with that beauty nuns have, sheltered from the world, from the sun by their wimples, wearing no makeup, yet which makes you wonder if it has some other source as well. She read her breviary for the first hour or so; but then took the folder of N.A.C. pamphlets from the pocket of the seat and read them attentively; and when the clouds cleared and there was a view to see, she looked at it eagerly.

The other girl was my seat-mate. She was dressed in the best of elegant, well-cut, unobtrusive taste, she was painted with professional skill. When we were in the air she took a typescript from her bag and began correcting it. As I had to look over her to see the mountains we were passing I could hardly help seeing that what she was correcting was an article on fashions. She put it away when she had done and read a small book instead. The title of it was *In Tune With the Infinite*.

Travelling by other means came later. Eventually I went a 200-mile journey by train. People told me I was mad. Travelling by train nearly killed *them*, they said. What would it do to me?

It gave me another enjoyable experience. It was sixteen years since I had been in a train. I noticed a few differences from that time. One now entered a carriage by a door in its side instead of from the platform at the end; the platform itself was now enclosed by a kind of bellows; the windows now opened by winding from the top instead of by clips from the bottom, and they no longer opened wide enough for you to put your head out and have it knocked off by a tunnel entrance; the tunnels near Wellington no longer filled the carriages with suffocating smoke (though they still did elsewhere) because that part of the line had been electrified. The biggest difference was in the length of it, only half as long as it was when I travelled on the same express as a child, and it now only ran twice a week instead of daily – so much difference had road travel made, and air travel to a smaller degree. And reading that within a few years all the provincial expresses would be replaced by railcars I felt I was just in time.

But most of the things I noticed I must have known before, and had forgotten. There was the distinctive motion of the train, the feeling of being dragged along willy-nilly, that the carriage hadn't the remotest idea itself where it was going but hung grimly to the tail of the one before and let happen to it what might, points, bridges, level-crossings with bells frantically ringing. There was the swaying, a surprising amount of swaying, and the metallic quality of the ride, and the clickety-clack, like a pulse measuring the energy of the train. I counted it by my watch – at one moment, in a rare long straight stretch, it beat eighty-eight to the minute, then as it climbed a hill dropped to forty-four; while in its cautious crossing of some of the older bridges it became scarcely perceptible. If I had known the distance between the joins in the rails I would have been able to work out the speed, I thought, comfortable in the knowledge that since I didn't know the distance my arithmetic wouldn't be put to such a test.

I had forgotten the excitement of looking from the window when the train was rounding a curve and seeing the engine belching smoke and feverishly pumping its pistons; I had forgotten the sight of a flock of sheep or a herd of cows showing their panic-stricken rumps as they streamed to the far end of a paddock – though now my memory was recalled I was sure it happened less often, that herds which stayed near the line placidly chewing their cuds were much more frequent than they were when I was young, and I wondered if they were now inheriting a lack of fear of railway trains. I had forgotten that in hilly country you don't get the same panoramic views of the countryside that you do from a car, since trains don't climb hills if they can help it, but wind through gullies and cuttings and tunnels. I had forgotten the sudden yawn of a train diving across a river, with nothing you can see between the carriage and the water. I had forgotten the stage presence guards develop, from having always to keep their balance in a moving train, while being watched by a carriageful of eyes. And I had forgotten the heat, and watched with compassion while a sick woman in the seat in front wilted under it, until she had to be revived with brandy from the flask I still carried in my pocket more for old times' sake than because I thought I might have need of it. I was sad to think there could be people so unwell that travelling could distress them.

I travelled by the inter-island steamer, and the first time I did it we had chosen a night when a southerly blew up and bent the trees low around our house before we set off and rocked the car as my father drove it down to Lyttelton from Evans Pass; and the ship rolled throughout the night, shifting my body in the bunk to the left and then to the right until I began to wonder if the world had ever been in equilibrium. Nor did the world right itself when I got on land. For several days I continued to roll rhythmically this way and that. During that same night the crew of a Lyttelton trawler were heroically rescuing the crew of a sinking yacht which had been competing in the race from Lyttelton to Wellington. Several of the other yachts went missing and some were never found. It was quite a beginning.

I stayed mostly with relatives on these longer journeys, fussed over, looked after.

'Do you like onion? Just tell me if you don't. What were you given a tongue for if you don't use it? Is that tea as you like it? Will you have some more custard? Are you quite sure there are enough blankets on your bed?'

I found it difficult to be dissatisfied enough to satisfy them.

Yet, though I enjoyed holidays, it was quite a time before I enjoyed *myself* on holiday. I was mortified to find how dependent I was on routine, how long it took me to get used to having morning tea at 9.30 instead of 10.30 and afternoon tea at 2.30

instead of 3.30. Every time I stayed away from home for a couple of years after I had begun travelling I found the strain of making these minute adjustments, and even of looking at a wallpaper with a different pattern, a window in a different place, of talking to different people, so acute that for several days after arriving at a new place I was in a state of complete exhaustion. After that I began to revive and the relative I was staying with would congratulate herself on the amazing difference their climate and her food and tender care had made to my health already. Always when I set out I was determined that this time I should not be overcome by this foolish restlessness, tiredness and depression, and always I was, until I had quite resigned myself to believing it was something I should always have to put up with. Then, quite suddenly, it was over; and after that, although I would still be fatigued if I did too much when I was away from home, I was no longer worried merely by being away from home.

But even though in those early days I couldn't escape from my vile body and its vile reactions, it still didn't keep me from absorbing impressions from outside. It may even have sharpened them. I noticed the small contrasts between the new districts and where I came from. I noticed the difference in the landscapes: the different shapes of hills, the impression which the little dried-up forlorn patches of bush still standing on the North Island hills give of a landscape unevenly flayed, whereas in most of the province of Canterbury there never was any bush, so its bareness – even where you will find that the grasses are imported – does not remind you of violence done to the country. And going further north I was conscious of the sudden subtle difference that appears half-way up the island, where the temperate gives way to the sub-tropical, which prompted one of the writers I lion-hunted to suggest that an enterprising Minister of Works should move Cook Strait to a line running roughly from New Plymouth to Whakatane, since it is now obviously in the wrong place.

Most of all what I noticed when I travelled, the thing which struck me most forcibly when I moved from one place to another, was that I had moved from one place to another. When I lived entirely in one place I had lost the feeling of place, of the limitations of space: living in one place I lived in infinity. It was only when I began to travel that I realised the evanescence of place, when I took a journey and one place gave way to another. I would be in a place where the sights and sounds so impressed themselves on my senses that I was sure they were there for all time – and the mere taking of a journey transformed them into an insubstantial, fading, memory.

I visited Tauranga one July. It might not have been the best time to be in Tauranga, but I thought it a pretty good time. The town itself didn't impress me much in July, except as a bustling country centre, but then New Zealand towns are seldom impressive as towns; and I was staying two or three miles out of town, on a hilltop in Judea – there was a Bethlehem, too, along the road. The citrus orchards were in full harvest, and sitting in the sun after a frost I looked down a slope of dark green bushes hung with shining balls, like over lush Christmas trees growing in rows. The sight evidently brought no great joy to the people who grew the trees. They agreed unanimously that citrus-farming didn't pay and that they were mugs to have taken it up; and they piled oranges into arms and pockets and lap until with the weight of them and the heat of the sun bouncing from the ground up at me I had no inclination and scarcely the ability to stir. Traffic swept along the main road at the back of the house between clay banks, a Maori boy and girl drifted past on bicycles and dismounted at the crossroads to smile at one another for a quarter of an hour before departing along different ways, a boy trotted by on a white horse and I crossed my fingers and waited for a dog; and the frost and the sun after it, the blue hills on the horizon and the green hills to hand, the oranges on the dark green trees, pressed themselves on the senses and filled the mind.

The whole world at that moment was Tauranga in July. But I left Tauranga and flew through a morning and afternoon in a great question mark, across to Gisborne and Napier, to Wellington and down the coast of the South Island to Christchurch. The scene changed from the green Bay of Plenty with the Rotorua lakes lying in a blue-grey mist on the right and the coastline sweeping away to East Cape on the left, changed to the dark bush of the Urewera, to the yellow hills of Hawke's Bay, and finally to the grey plains of Canterbury – grey of ploughed fields, dormant grass and leafless trees. At any other time Christchurch is brilliantly coloured, but in mid-winter the ground is bare and what plants there are have stopped growing, and often enough – as in the week after I returned home – the grey becomes greyer from reflecting a leaden sky. It may have its own beauty, but I can never find much to admire in the colours that accompany cold weather, unless they're a long way off like snow on distant mountains.

And yet that chill drabness obliterated entirely those green and orange hillsides, or at least reduced them to a faint image in the memory and very feeble the memory seemed after the sight. The drab conquered because it was there to be seen and the bright retreated because it was no longer before the eyes; and Tauranga faded into a sidestream of a memory whose main flow was in other places. People asked if I had had a good holiday and I told them enthusiastically I had, knowing I had, yet wishing I still felt the enthusiasm I expressed. I knew I'd had a good holiday almost by hearsay, as if someone had told me – someone whose word I didn't doubt, certainly; but the lukewarmness of the response seemed a betrayal.

Memory, I knew, had its revenge later on, when in a few selected instances it would turn itself into nostalgia to plague and delight with an enlarged picture of what never was. I was used to that trick of memory: mine had been given plenty of opportunity to indulge it. Its weakness in the immediate aftermath of a journey was what I found startling.

Fourteen

My most recent journey was back to Green Lane as an outpatient to see my old friends, to let them take X-rays and electrocardiographs and blood tests, to listen in, to gloat over one of their most successful guinea-pigs. Most of the doctors I had known were still around, some of the sisters and many of the orderlies; but the junior nurses had long since been called to higher spheres or had married or taken trips overseas. I realised how the time had been passing when I heard myself referred to several times as 'one of our earliest Blalock cases'. I hadn't got over thinking of myself as one of their latest.

No one can live on his operation all his life, although if it was spectacular enough it can give him a pretty good run. Fame based even on a heart operation is a fading asset. Heart operations are still not quite commonplace, they still have their interest. (I wonder, by the way, why operations and diseases of the thorax are still thought respectable, even a shade romantic, while those of the abdomen are a trifle obscene?) But they no longer arouse quite the same breathless excitement they once did. They are becoming accepted. What news value they still have is mostly reserved for operations which actually penetrate inside the heart and there is little left for those which, although considered heart operations, are performed on the arteries outside the heart. The Blalock operation itself it now superseded in most cases by a newer technique. Surgeons now go more directly to the seat of the trouble and have progressed some way towards an actual cure, instead of merely providing relief. As a medical curiosity I've become almost passé. I live in another town now, too, where the people I meet did not know me when I was bedridden, and to them the limitations I still have must be more obvious than the new life I've been given.

Even my own bright new vision of the world shows signs of fading at times. I no longer see things every moment with the same new eyes I did. The penalty of growing well is that you get used to it and can live for days without constantly thinking this is me, I am doing these incredible things. But then some stimulus reminds you and it all comes back. I have not yet stopped improving, but the improvement is slower, though more steady, than it was at first. Advances are measured in years rather than in weeks, and they only slowly modify the life I've evolved, which by co-operating with my remaining disability leaves me scarcely conscious of the things I can't yet do.

I do not go out to work, but I write and type for several hours a day at home and earn a few cheques, a few brickbats, a few bouquets. I do my few chores around the house, I pull out an odd weed or two from the garden; I visit, I go to the pictures, I do business in the township, I lend a little voluntary labour to the local library, degrading self-respecting books fresh from the shop into mere library books and listening to the latest news of Mrs M.'s Barbara and Mrs R.'s Barbara and Mrs W.'s Barbara, hearing Mrs O'L. praise Ireland and tell us about O'Connor, O'Casey, O'Faolain and O'Flaherty. All of them Mrs, because I am an outsider in what for other men is a dormitory suburb, where the only males to be seen apart from a few serving behind shop counters are the white-headed ones who queue at the Post Office every month for their pensions.

I have settled into the community, though I can hardly persuade myself that I am of much use to it. I am certainly more use to my family up than in bed; they are relieved not only of some physical burdens, but also – what I think was the worst part – of the constant anxiety which I had given them going steadily downhill. The change was not all benefit to them: it is no longer possible for my mother, when she receives an invitation she has no wish to accept, to say, 'I'm so very sorry, I'd love to come, but Dennis isn't at all well and I really can't leave him.' But even so this is some slight comfort when I ask myself, objectively, what is the value of heart operations, when my intellect begins to have stern Malthusian doubts as to whether surgeons are justified in using their skill and the country its money to prolong the lives of the unfit in a world where there are too many mouths to feed already; when I wonder what good it can do anyone to postpone one person's trip to his Maker (for how long nobody knows), when people are still dying all around and we are all likely to be vaporised by hydrogen bombs some day soon in any case. But I take no real notice of such arguments. Although I may not be able to construct any satisfactory rationalisation to justify my continued presence in the world I don't intend to apologise for staying around.

No one knows exactly why anyone should be a blue-baby, and during the years I was ill it never occurred to me to question why it should happen to *me*, the question which fiction-writers suppose to preoccupy such as I was. It might have been an interesting point to speculate about, but it seemed to me as essentially unanswerable, and therefore meaningless, as to ask why I was born a New Zealander rather than an Eskimo. One is involved in mankind and cannot escape the penalties which that fact often entails. I did not feel hardly done by that fate or God's Providence (I know which I prefer to call it) should have chosen one rather than another situation in which I was to make my life; but when I was enabled to change my state in life, I changed it, and was content. One knows what one knows and if the reason expresses doubts that to be alive is better than to be dead or that to be well is better than to be ill, then reason is a fool.

Certainly the life of an invalid has its own private richness, although it is more obvious to me now than it was then. Some neighbours of ours when I was a child had a movie projector which was wound by hand. If you wanted Charlie Chaplin to walk faster you wound the handle faster, to slow him down you wound slower. The effect of getting well was like accelerating that machine. So many more events happened that I could no longer give to each the attention I once could. I had to learn to make my view of life from a synthesis of many happenings rather than an analysis of a few. But, as one looks back with regret on childhood and adolescence after they are safely over without really wishing to be back there, I had no desire to return to the earlier phase even in the first breathless beginning of the acceleration when I felt at times that I was being hit over the head with event after event, and wondered at my foolishness in wanting to live in a world which often seemed as lunatic as anything in *City Lights* or *Modern Times.* A withdrawal into my shell long enough to collect my scattered wits fixed that trouble; then I would find myself longing to be back to carry on the fight. And if I retained certain habits from my earlier days, among them a liking for doses of solitude, that merely showed I was one continuing person. I couldn't claim to have been made into someone else by my experiences; the heart operation wrought no fundamental change of heart; there was no point in time to which I could look back and discern a change from someone who was not I to someone who was. I remained I, all along the way.

Only now I am I in the world instead of out of it, and I am glad to be here. I read Pascal and learn from him that human life is misery and wretchedness; and I know he speaks the truth. I read many of our New Zealand writers and learn from them that New Zealand is a dreary (some say a drizzly) wasteland, in which we try to escape from our puritan consciences, which we have not the courage to abandon though we no longer have faith in anything to sustain them, by the aid of six o'clock swills and the banknote dreams of the Totalisator Agency Board. I admire these writers, and I know they write the truth. Yet heresy keeps breaking through, my senses keep denying the truths which reason preaches to them; grace is denied, and however much I try, I cannot find life miserable and wretched and I do not find New Zealand drizzly.

My way in the world has only yet begun. I have many things to see and to know and to do and to grow. How it will all be I do not know, but I know how it has been, and that is enough.

Notes

The numbers refer to pages.

[8] The determined editor was Alun Richards.

[17] The minister of health was Mabel Howard.

[28] Miss J.: Muriel Johnston.

[32] The radiologist 'descended . . . from one of the city's best-known statues': George Rolleston.

[33] Young T.: Howard Tripp.

[38] The Sister in Charge of the Cardio-Surgical Clinic was Mary Smaill.

[40] This IQ test was part of a research project into the effect of long-term cyanosis (blueness from shortage of oxygen) on intelligence. It indicates the culture of the time that even in the relatively open environment of Green Lane I was not told this, let alone asked for my permission or told the result. The conclusion of the study was that there was very little effect. The average IQ of all cases was 99; the range about what you would find in the general population. (Edward H. Roche and Anthony H. G. Roche, *Green Lane Saga*, Auckland, 1983, p.45.)

[54] Mr R.: Douglas Robb.

[56] Mr N.: Rowan Nicks.

[56] (Original footnote: 'Only it wasn't Browning'.) The name was Swinburn.

[64] 'Physiotherapy is very backward in America.' This sentence was omitted from the American edition.

[65] The 'slight, fair girl' was Zoe Greenhough. Seventeen years later I married her.

[73] The visitor of uncertain age was Vi Blair; she was the subject of a chapter in a later book of mine, *Arguing With My Grandmother*.

[80] The Presbyterian minister: Alan Brash.

[85] This use of the word 'convert [to one's own use]' in the sense of 'steal' puzzled the editor of the American edition. She changed it to 'covet'.

[89] Of the speakers at the protest rally, the man I took to be a lawyer was Lincoln Efford, who was not a lawyer, the lecturer in economics Wolfgang Rosenberg, the 'furious housewife' May Furey, the Marxist trade union secretary A. B. Grant, the writer of letters-to-the-editor John Johnson, the Anglican clergyman David Taylor and the Presbyterian clergyman Malcolm Wilson.

[102] The Bishop was Alwyn Warren, newly elected Anglican Bishop of Christchurch; the shop was Beaths; see *Hebrews* 12:1.

[111] 'The poet who looked like a poet' was James K. Baxter; the man in the duffel coat (a garment so new to New Zealand I did not know its name), Allen Curnow. Baxter's address was published as *Recent Trends in New Zealand Poetry*.

[112] The rural sage: Oliver Duff.

[113] The Auckland novelist: Frank Sargeson.

[114] The poet 'who didn't look like a poet' was Louis Johnson: the reference is to his first wife, Pat.

[115] 'The up-and-coming youngster.' (Original footnote: 'Or one of them. There were actually two, but as they thought and spoke alike I have kept the person singular.') The two I rolled into one were Robert Chapman and Jonathan Bennett, who were selecting poems for what became *An Anthology of New Zealand Verse*, published by Oxford University Press in 1956. Their more conservative counterpart was Donald Anderson.

[117] The Talks Officer: Arnold Wall.

[124] The 'article by the Vicar on Muslim beliefs regarding the last day' appeared in the *Akaroa Mail*.

[128] The storm that overtook the yacht race from Lyttelton to Wellington was the subject of Ruth France's sadly neglected novel, *The Race*.

[133] Margaret McEldowney (my sister-in-law), Margaret Robertson and Ellen Wallace did all have school-age daughters named Barbara; May O'Leary was another subject of my book *Arguing With My Grandmother*.